WOMAN
REMOVE
THY
VEIL

by: Barbara Cassada

Scripture quotations marked (PET or The Message) are taken from the *PETERSON TRANSLATION, THE MESSAGE,* © 1993, 1994, 1995 by Eugene H. Peterson, NavPress, P.O. Box 35001, Colorado Springs, CO 80935

Published by:

Tome Publishing
909 Brown School Rd
Maryville TN 37804
(865) 310-1805

Cover Design by: Deborah Taylor
Photography by: Kenneth Davey
Model: Roxana Davey

Chapter		Page

Barbara Cassada is one of the most intelligent persons I know. She knows how to do her research, and is faithful in trying to let all the Scripture speak for itself. She is not only highly intelligent, she is also a person of bold faith. She and her husband Bill are being powerfully used to equip the saints for the work of ministry. They are servants of God who took early retirement (Bill), and who left a great career just short of being vested (Barbara) in order to say "yes" to God's call on their lives. They have also caught the fire for impartation from me and are faithfully multiplying what I have been doing. They traveled with me for about a year and were found most faithful in being willing to serve. One thing you will find about Barbara is that you won't have to guess what she thinks or where she is at regarding her viewpoints. She is not one who plays it safe by hiding behind presenting all the various views on a subject without committing herself to one of the views. She has never been a "middle of the road", "play it safe" type of person.

Rather, she has been a radical, totally sold out to Jesus type, disciple. I believe she will be in her writing what she is in person, an "in your face" person asking you "what do you believe?" I doubt that you will be able to read anything that Barbara writes without being challenged by her, and I believe also by the Holy Spirit. She comes across in true prophetic type ministry, not with the gentleness of the priestly - pastoral office; that is who she is and how she writes. So hang on to your seat as you begin to read. You may get angry with her writing, but you certainly will not be bored. I thank God for Barbara, a woman of courage, faith, insight, prophetic gifting, and anointing for preaching.

Randy Clark
International Evangelist and
Founder of Global Awakening Ministries

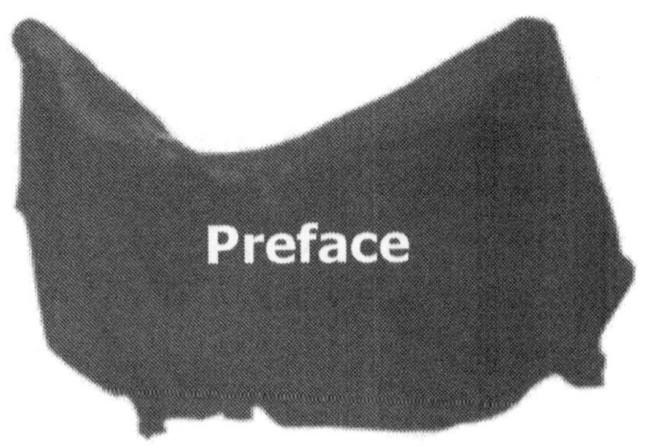

Are we in the last of the last days? Perhaps. It seems like the Spirit of the Lord is moving on the face of the earth in awesome, and unprecedented ways. As we have traveled around the world ministering, we find like hearts seeking God in humility, desperation, passion, and with exuberant, uninhibited worship. It seems the earth is in renewal, the forerunner of revival. With revival comes healing – healing of the nations, people groups, and individuals' hearts from past wounds, as well as physical healings of all types of infirmity. With revival comes reconciliation – reconciling of the hearts of the fathers with the hearts of the children, reconciling of the races, reconciling of different theological viewpoints, and reconciling of generations. As we approach the soon return of our Lord Jesus Christ, the hearts of men and women everywhere are laying aside perceived truths to seek together a more intimate relationship with the One to whom we are accountable. We are finding people falling in love with Jesus and pursuing His presence in continuous, harmonious heart cries. A love for the brethren in the body and a love for the not-yet-saved is filling the hearts of people around the world who are experiencing a new, refreshing, and major outpouring of love from the Father.

As we move into revival, we pray for, with hopeful expectation, the reconciliation of the world to Christ and to each other. This book examines only one aspect of reconciliation, that of men and women in the body of Christ. It seems, as we move forward in history, one of the serious breaches in Christendom is left primarily intact — that of women's roles in the church. As we move into a freedom in Christ, the subject seems to come up more and more as God pours out His Spirit on His handmaidens around the world. Yet a large segment of the church, in attempting to address the issue, continues to go back to a theology of old.

We have been in many churches where some members of the leadership have questioned the pastor about my "right" to speak in their church. Because of the message we bring – salvation, healing, and deliverance – from a non-denominational perspective, we have been blessed to minister in many mainline denominational churches. But in a lot of cases, eyebrows were raised, even though the power of God was manifest and people were saved, set free, and healed. In my secular position as an air traffic controller before going into fulltime ministry, I encountered a degree of male prejudice. However, in that male dominated profession, as my abilities were recognized I earned the respect of my male counterparts. I was surprised to find this same prejudice in a large part of the church of Jesus Christ, and the anointing didn't seem to counter that prejudice. This caused me to stop and ponder just what Jesus really did for the world. Are we all free? Are we all in Christ? Are we all one together in Him, one body, and many members? So I set out to find the truth.

Like most Christian women I have spoken with on the issue, we all wanted to be in God's perfect will, obedient to His Word, and not in rebellion in any way. Yet as we tried to comply with what we believed was the truth about submission and women's roles in the body we had to be honest with ourselves. Down deep inside a voice was crying out for equality and justice; the way submission was being taught grated on the inside while we tried to be obedient on the outside. I came to the conclusion that the Spirit of God who indwells all those called by His name was speaking deep within our hearts to seek out the truth. If He anoints us, can we deny that anointing? Are we truly in rebellion when we hear and comply with the voice of the Spirit? This posed questions to ponder, search out, and have answered by God.

When Moses descended the mountain, the people asked him to cover his face because it was too bright to look upon. The faces of half of the bride, half of the body of Christ, have been covered with a veil of tradition. We have been covered in order not to offend. But the Groom is coming to kiss the bride, not through a veil, but face to face. Women carry the glory of God as do men. Should we put a veil over it as Moses did?

2 Corinthians 3:12-14

Since we have such [glorious] hope (such joyful and confident expectation), we speak very freely *and* openly *and* fearlessly. Nor [do we act] like Moses, who put a veil over his face so that the Israelites might not gaze upon the finish of the vanishing [splendor which had been upon it]. In fact, their minds were grown hard *and* calloused [they had become dull and had lost the power of understanding]; for until this present day, when the Old Testament (the old covenant) is being read, that same veil still lies [on their hearts], not being lifted [to reveal] that in Christ it is made void *and* done away. (Amplified Bible)

If men and women are circumcised in their hearts by the redemptive work of Christ, then the veil over all our hearts must be rent. The sword pierced Jesus' heart[1] as He hung on the cross, tearing away the veil that separated us from God and from each other. Our traditions continue to repair the veil and reestablish it over our hearts so that we cannot see the splendor of the glory of God shining forth from His bride. We must focus on God and the purpose and destiny He has for His bride, not on legalism and tradition. If God asks us to do something contrary to the accepted norm in the church, should we not obey Him rather than tradition?

Are we not being asked the same question as Peter was asked before the rulers and elders of the people in Jerusalem?

Acts 4:7

And when they had set them in the midst, they asked, "By what power or by what name have you done this?"

Women have been accused of ministering under the power of Satan, or at least one of his minions. And yet when we see salvations, healings, and deliverances in the name of Jesus, we must answer with Peter:

Acts 4:8-10

Then Peter, filled with the Holy Spirit, said to them, "Rulers of the people and elders of Israel: If we this day are judged for a good deed *done* to a helpless man, by what means he has been made well, let it be known to you all, and to all the people of Israel, that by the name of Jesus Christ of Nazareth, whom you crucified, whom God raised from the dead, by Him this man stands here before you whole."

If the ends do not justify the means as professed by some (quoted in Chapter 6), and God does not give His approval to women ministering the Gospel, what hope have we? Does 2 Corinthians Chapter 3 only apply to men? If so, does any of the Scripture apply to women? If we are commanded by men not to teach, then should we not join with Peter in saying:

Acts 4:18-19

And they called them and commanded them not to speak at all nor teach in the name of Jesus. But Peter and John answered and said to them, "Whether it is right in the sight of God to listen to you more than to God, you judge."

My husband and the Lord know my heart is to serve God, become more like Jesus, and be pleasing to the Father. I thank the Lord for giving me a godly husband, with whom I can stand along side, and who stands along side me in teaching, preaching, praying, and seeking God. It is because Bill recognizes the anointing

God has deposited within me and encourages my full participation in ministry that I have such [glorious] hope (such joyful and confident expectation), and, therefore, speak very freely *and* openly *and* fearlessly (Heb. 3:12 Amplified).

I pray that this book blesses and challenges you, and may God bring you more fully into the intimacy that He shares with His unveiled bride.

In Service of the King(dom),
Barbara Cassada

---

[1] John 19:34. Jesus heart was indeed pierced as evidenced by the water, which came from His side along with the blood. This is expounded on in Chapter 2.

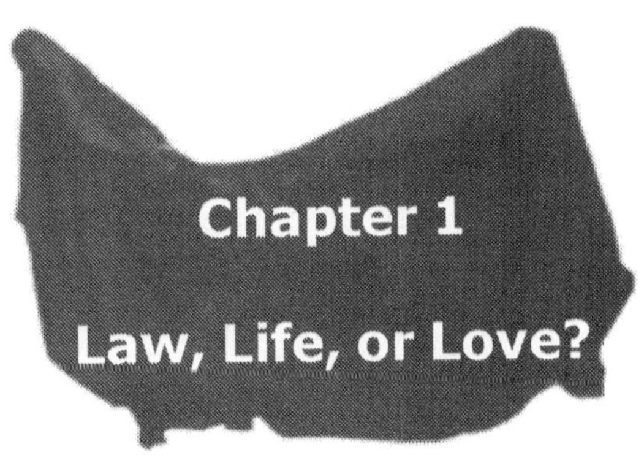

The Holy Bible: is it a book of laws, a book of life, or a book of love? Is this a process, progression, pilgrimage, or perspective?

God-fearing parents raise their children with rules and parameters out of love and concern. The children, of course, don't see the reasons for the restrictions until they begin to mature. Mom and Dad give rules. Don't do this, do that. Just to see if we can learn to obey? (The Law)

As a young Christian I saw the Holy Bible as a book of laws. And I recognize a reluctance in some people to accept Jesus Christ as Lord because their perception is the same. I will have to give up my life, all that I am, and all that I enjoy if I become a Christian. We can't get past the dos and don'ts. Our perspective is in the outer court at the brazen altar. Jesus cleansed us of our sins, removed the consequences of disobeying the law, but we still see the law and continue to go back to the brazen altar.

Our view in the outer court begins to change, however, as we are drawn to the structure up ahead, the tabernacle veiled in mystery. We sense a longing to know more and begin to move toward the tent that holds the secrets of His presence. Having accepted Christ, getting past our initial reluctance to bow our knee to a law we are not sure we can comply with, our view begins to change. We learn of what He did for us and why, and we begin to see the Bible as a book of life. Just as a child begins to recognize that mom and dad have laid down the rules, not to control us, but to protect us from the evils of this world, so we begin to see God, the loving Father, not God, the strict disciplinarian. "Don't run out into the street," becomes not a command to prevent us from having fun, but a warning of danger should we choose to disregard parental wisdom.

We begin to experience the life that flows from the Word of God. As He protects us, nurtures us, teaches us, and transforms us we begin to enjoy the power and authority of His life flowing in and through us. We see circumstances change as we begin to trust in a God we cannot see but now know exists. We have gone beyond the outer court into the Holy Place. We find ourselves at the Golden Lampstand of anointing manifesting His gifts and producing fruits as we learn to walk in the Spirit. Illumination increases as we spend time studying the Word. We begin to eat of the bread of life from the table of shewbread and find that we walk differently. Our outlook, physical well being, and worldly passions have all changed. We begin to know Him as our provider, healer, and friend as we learn to pray, praise, and worship at the altar of incense. Our perspective has once again changed as we progress further and further into the Presence. The more we grow the more we realize there is something else, something missing. This is not all there is. A veil hangs before us and we begin to experience a hunger to know what lies beyond, a hunger that cannot be satisfied in the outer chamber of the Holy Place. What lies beyond calls us as deep calls unto deep. We are growing, maturing, and His transforming power is changing us from what we once were to what He desires us to be—a bride.

Finally we begin to experience the Word of God, the Bible, not as a book of laws or even just a book of life. We find it always was a book of love—from cover to cover a message of enduring, unconditional, passionate, and selfless love. That love flowing from the throne of grace is calling us, drawing us into the Holy of Holies. It's there that the final transformation occurs. We are being changed from glory to glory (2 Cor. 3:18) into the image of Christ — a bride comparable to Him, without spot and wrinkle. This is a love story of eternal proportions. A king, God, Creator, eternally perfect being, having no needs or wants, chose for some inexplicable reason to have a desire. That desire was for a bride. His plan required a birth, death, and resurrection. He chose to be the one to die for the bride He loved. What greater love could anyone experience?

A few have made it to this ultimate revelation. The mystics knew it to be a love story. They found in their solitude the communion of spirit that drove them continually into the arms of the lover of their souls. Most of us never get there. Perhaps it is because we are locked in our misunderstandings of scripture, our false ideas of what it really means, our reluctance to enter all the way in to the most intimate relationship imaginable. Our natural perversions prevent our spiritual growth because we can't seem to "get it".

The Father continued to reveal the plan over and over again. The scriptures cry out with the love story of the ages. Israel was chosen—a prophetic representation of a spiritual reality. She would represent humanity in her relationship with God. By studying God's dealing with her we can better understand His plans for us. Isaiah, Jeremiah, Joel, John, Revelation, and many other books of the Bible speak of the bride. Through the Old and New Testament there is the language of intimacy in marriage. We can know and be known in the Holy of Holies, the intimate place where the groom's love is manifest fully to His bride.

> 1 Corinthians 8:3
>
> But if one loves God truly [with affectionate reverence, prompt obedience, and grateful recognition of His blessing], he is known by God [recognized as worthy of His intimacy and love, and he is owned by Him]. (Amplified)

This is the language of the Bible. Until we gain access to the Holy of Holies and know the heart of the Father, until we recognize the Bible as a book of love, we will continue to interpret scripture with a legalistic flavor that keeps us in bondage. Whom the Son sets free is free indeed (John 8:36). He has indeed set us free. But we choose, because of our own agendas, biases, and misunderstandings to put boundaries around that freedom and rather than the chains of love that bind us to Christ, we embrace chains of bondage that keep us from the inner chamber. It is time to break out of our self-imposed restrictions and allow God to be manifest in and through His bride. Let the world see Him, in and through us, His bride. If Jesus is to manifest His glory through both genders, then we must look to the Cross of Christ as our ministerial focus, understanding that the Cross nullified the curse, washed us clean, and removed the veil that we might commune with our lover face to face.

The brazen altar — a type and shadow of the Cross where we began our Christian journey — is a bloody place of sacrifice. It is a place where our sins are forgiven. So many camp out there in the outer court. Sins forgiven. Why? To avoid the fires of hell and enter into heaven upon our physical death? A myopic view of the Cross — the awesome place where ultimate love was revealed. What held Jesus to that tree except the incredible love that He had for a bride that was to be. For the joy set before Him, He endured the punishment due us (Hebrews 12:2), seeing the ultimate end of the Father's plan. With eternal perspective He chose to die for her that she might begin the journey from orphan girl to a King's bride. He died to redeem her. He returned to His kingdom to prepare a place for her and sent His Spirit to prepare her for that place.

We must study all scripture through the Cross of Christ, the ultimate demonstration of love. The Bible is a love story from Genesis to Revelation. We have for centuries allowed our theologies, doctrines, and perspectives of what the Bible truly says to be influenced by what others have said it means. Some have had a piece of divine revelation that revolutionized the body and moved her forward in her journey toward the Holiest Place. But because they had a piece, we accepted everything they said as revelatory truth. We have allowed our teachers to be persons influenced by their own prejudices and skewed interpretations of scripture. The Bible is clear when it says that we need that no man teach us. Not that we don't need teachers. We surely do. But it is the Holy Spirit who brings revelation of the truth. He is the one who wraps the scripture in the Father's love, and delivers the package to our hearts. It is by His ministration that we are transformed. Truth is beauty. He is truth. Humanity's corrupt nature perverts the Word and we stand in the outer court seeing a book of laws. Through the eyes of the law we see words in scripture like authority, covering, submission, and headship from a legalistic perspective. We find them to be hard words; but in our desire to please God, we attempt to comply with the words from our outer court immaturity.

It is time for the bride of Christ to mature into her role of co-laborer (Mark 16:20), advancing the Kingdom of God and displacing the kingdom of Satan. We can only achieve His goals when we set aside race, generational, theological, cultural, class, and gender issues and begin to understand His purpose for us all. We are to become one in Him. Paul tells us that marriage is a mystery, two becoming one flesh, but that he speaks of Christ and the Church (Eph 5:31-32). We are corporately the bride. I have witnessed men being transformed as they approached that intimate place in the Holy of Holies. It seemed that the closer they moved toward the Father's heart, the more apparent the bride became in them individually. Sensitivity, passion, tenderness, and unashamed emotion are revealed as men choose their place in the bride. Selfish pride, with its outworking in a need to dominate, control, manipulate, rule, and lord over, vanished in the place of awesome intimacy with a groom whose love for His bride is unconditional, unfailing, and all encompassing.

Would that more of the Church would understand the love Jesus has for her. It is never controlling, dominating, or manipulating. His love is always tender, wooing, nurturing, and passionate. We are temples of His most Holy Spirit and He is ever zealous for us (John 2:17). But our fallen nature tends to mask the revelation of Christ's love with legalism and worldly, soulish interpretation that leaves little room for a mutual co-laboring.

Hierarchy, Yes or No?

Most of my research on the roles of women in the church has led in one of two directions. Either Christ totally redeemed women into equality with men in all areas and the gender issue is no longer relevant, or God did indeed create a hierarchy when He formed man first and woman thereafter. It is interesting to note that all the research I have uncovered advocating the latter is based on Genesis 3:16.

Genesis 3:16

> To the woman He said: "I will greatly multiply your
> sorrow and your conception;
> In pain you shall bring forth children;
> Your desire *shall be* for your husband,
> **And he shall rule over you.**" (Emphasis mine)

Interesting, because this scripture comes subsequent to the fall. Therefore, it is relevant to the consequences that resulted from sin not to the Cross that redeemed us from sin. The body of Christ has only one head, Jesus Christ Himself. He is the one who rules and reigns. The Spirit of God that indwells the believer is quite capable of leading each individual down the path God chooses for them. He rules over individual hearts; man does not rule man under God's divine order. Instead, we are accountable to each other as we submit one to another in the harmony of Christ. Maturity leads immaturity into growth until we all come to the stature of Christ. Only as a consequence of sin does one person attempt to control another. It is the fallen nature that rules itself and thus others. The sin of Satan, attempting to elevate himself above God, permeates the depths of our fallen soul. Only through redemption and repentance can we release the need to dominate others and accept the unconditional lordship of Jesus Christ.

Robert E. Billings, Jr. states in his article "*Should Women Speak in the Church*" that Paul's restriction on women "is a result of God's created order and the fact that the woman was deceived first."[1] He states unequivocally: "Eve is told that Adam is to rule over her. Therefore, she was to submit to him."[2] Note that he implies that Adam was deceived since woman was "deceived first". Paul tells us clearly in 1 Timothy 2:14 that Adam was in no way deceived. But we will talk about this later. Let us for now examine the creation order.

It is generally understood by most theologians that Chapter 1 of Genesis provides an overview of the sequence of creation. In this Chapter God creates mankind.

Genesis 1:27-28

So God created man in His *own* image; in the image of God He created him; male and female He created them. Then God blessed them, and God said to them, "Be fruitful and multiply; fill the earth and subdue it; have dominion over the fish of the sea, over the birds of the air, and over every living thing that moves on the earth."

Notice that he blessed *them* and gave *them* dominion. Genesis Chapter 2 goes into more detail about God's special creation.

Genesis 2:5-8, 15-25

5 For the Lord God had not caused it to rain on the earth, and *there was* no man to till the ground;6 but a mist went up from the earth and watered the whole face of the ground.7 And the Lord God formed man *of* the dust of the ground, and breathed into his nostrils the breath of life; and man became a living being.8 The Lord God planted a garden eastward in Eden, and there He put the man whom He had formed.

15 Then the Lord God took the man and put him in the garden of Eden to tend and keep it.16 And the Lord God commanded the man, saying, "Of every tree of the garden you may freely eat;17 "but of the tree of the knowledge of good and evil you shall

not eat, for in the day that you eat of it you shall surely die."

18 And the LORD God said, "*It is* not good that man should be alone; I will make him a helper comparable to him."19 Out of the ground the LORD God formed every beast of the field and every bird of the air, and brought *them* to Adam to see what he would call them. And whatever Adam called each living creature, that *was* its name.20 So Adam gave names to all cattle, to the birds of the air, and to every beast of the field. But for Adam there was not found a helper comparable to him.21 And the LORD God caused a deep sleep to fall on Adam, and he slept; and He took one of his ribs, and closed up the flesh in its place.22 Then the rib which the LORD God had taken from man He made into a woman, and He brought her to the man.23 And Adam said: "This *is* now bone of my bones And flesh of my flesh; She shall be called Woman, Because she was taken out of Man." 24 Therefore a man shall leave his father and mother and be joined to his wife, and they shall become one flesh.25 And they were both naked, the man and his wife, and were not ashamed.

God creates His man and places him in a special garden with instructions to tend and keep it. Then He makes an interesting statement. He says that it is not good that man should be alone. Therefore He will make another creation that is comparable to the man — one who is like unto him, equal to, the same as. The New Bible Dictionary states that "God resolved to provide 'a helper fit for him' ('ēzer kᵉneḡdô, Gn. 2:18, 20, lit. 'a helper as in front of him', *i.e.* 'a *helper corresponding* to him')."[3] This statement by God does not make the woman in any way inferior or subjected to man. It makes her an equal partner in the subjugation of the rest of the created world. The fascinating part, however, occurs in the very next action. God immediately brings all the animals to Adam to name. It is beyond lunacy to think that God was somehow searching for a mate for Adam among the animals. So why would He bring the creatures to Adam to name immediately after stating the need for a helper comparable to Adam?

The answer is obvious in its simplicity. God was not looking for a mate for Adam among the animals. He had already purposed what He was going to do. The centrality of the Bible is the Cross of Christ — a redeemer who comes to save a people that He would have as His bride. She was always in the Father's heart. Adam and Eve would be the first to emulate the relationship that the Father had chosen for Christ and His church. Eve was not an afterthought. She was always preeminent, uppermost in the heart of the Father. But Adam did not yet have the revelation of the Father's plan. He didn't miss having a bride because he never had one. There was no partner for him and we have a saying that "you don't miss what you never had." A desire and passion for a mate must first be birthed in Adam's heart or he wouldn't understand what Eve's role was to be. Adam needed to come to the realization that he had no one like himself. He must have a revelation of his own inadequacy, his incompleteness, and his inability to carry out the command of God by himself.

By bringing the animals to Adam, God was demonstrating the "law of Genesis". Each part of creation — animals, birds, fish, and plants — all produced after their own kind according to the law of God. Only after seeing the "law of Genesis" enacted among the animals would he begin to realize that he was alone. God showed Adam that everything He created produced after its own kind; that it took two of every animal to produce offspring. In order to multiply and fill the earth, Adam would need someone like himself. Adam could not be fruitful and multiply as the Lord commanded him to do because he was the only one of his kind. As he began to recognize his aloneness, a desire for a partner was born in him. When he realized that there was no one like himself that could help him fulfill the command of God, that he was the only one, then God brought forth Eve.

It is no different now than it was then. Only when we realize our aloneness and need for a savior, only when the understanding of our inability to go it alone is manifest can the Father truly penetrate our hearts with the revelation of His love. Our desperation and hunger draw the lover of our soul and we see Him for the first time as the fulfiller of our need. And so it was with Adam. He began to understand God's plan and a desire and passion for a mate was birthed. This is so plainly evident in Adam's response when he first sees Eve. The Living Bible says it this way:

Genesis 2:23

"This is it!" Adam exclaimed. "She is part of my own bone and flesh! Her name is 'woman' because she was taken out of a man."

Adam immediately recognized his helpmate — the one like him, the one comparable to him, and the one who could help him fulfill the command of God. God took Eve from the side of Adam not the head, the stomach, the foot, but the side. Not because she was less or inferior, but because this prophetic act represented the bride of Christ being taken from the heart of the Father. The word for rib in the Hebrew is tselă {**tsay-law'**} which comes from the root word **TWOT** meaning side, chamber (chambers or cells-of temple structure), and rib. A chamber of the heart perhaps? When our Lord hung on the Cross, His side was pierced and from the wound flowed blood and water. A sac called the pericardium surrounds the human heart. This sac is filled with water and protects the heart from shock that occurs in falls or hard blows to the body. When Jesus' side was pierced the pericardium was breached, indicating that the spear penetrated to His heart, causing water and blood to flow from His side. The bride of Christ was birthed (redeemed) by the blood that flowed from His side. The Church was born from the heart of the Father at the moment of Christ's death on the Cross. What an incredibly beautiful picture of our redemption. Jesus gave Himself for a bride that was to be, and from His side the Father took her. She will be presented to her groom without spot or wrinkle on that glorious day.

When Adam saw Eve he knew the intent in the Father's heart and recognized Eve as the one who was comparable to him. Now he was complete and together they could do what God commanded them to do. Adam could only produce fruit with and through another like himself, the same yet different, his completion, a co-laborer in the Kingdom. (Jesus Christ was the first born among many and He chooses to produce fruit with and through the "ecclesia", the church, His bride, co-laboring together with Him. 1 Cor. 3:9) Moreover, since Adam had not yet fallen, he had the mind of God. Prophesying God's plan for man and woman he spoke:

Genesis 2:24

Therefore a man shall leave his father and mother
and be joined to his wife, and they shall become
one flesh.

We, as members of the body of Christ, part of His
Church, learning intimacy as a bride, are to put on Christ,
be clothed in Christ (Galatians 3:27), be transformed
into the image of the glory of Christ (2 Cor. 3:18). In
other words, become one with Christ as Adam and Eve
became one flesh. Paul speaks of the mystery of marriage being Christ and the Church. Can we have any
doubt when viewed in the light of scripture that the
Father's plan was to have a bride for the Son? God intended that man and woman together would take back
His earth and walk in the power and anointing that He
would bestow on them. He also knew what was coming and it was His intent that we walk out the relationship that would represent to the world Christ and His
bride, the Church.

When the fall occurred, mankind's nature changed
aligning itself with God's enemy. The "god of self" now
dominated our being. When God spoke to Eve it was
not to pronounce a curse upon her, but to inform her of
the consequences of the sin. Humankind would now be
self-centered, self-aware, self-preserving, self-conscious,
self-promoting, self-indulging, and in all other ways selfish. Man would rule over woman from this point forward, not because it was God's plan but because it was
in man's sinful, selfish nature to do so. F. F. Bruce dis-
cusses this in his book *A Mind for What Matters.*

It is in the fall narrative, not in the creation narratives, that superiority of the one sex over the other is first mentioned. And here it is not an inherent superiority, but one that is exercised by force. The Creator's words to Eve, 'your desire shall be for your husband, and he will rule over you' (Gen. 3:1), mean that, in our sinful human condition, the man exploits the woman's natural proclivity towards him to dominate and subjugate her. Subjugation of woman, in fact, is a symptom of man's fallen nature.[4]

The Cross of Christ restored mankind to the Father's original purpose, redeeming us from the consequences of sin. The sin nature, which continues to raise its ugly head, can only be thwarted by the Cross and the love that was demonstrated thereon. To understand what we are dealing with in this subjugation of women, we must more fully comprehend what really happened in the Garden of Eden.

Chapter Two Notes

[1] Billings, Robert E. Jr. Should Women Speak in the Church (1 Aug. 2000): p 7. Online. Internet 13 May 2001.
[2] IBID. p 6.
[3] The New Bible Dictionary, (Wheaton, Illinois: Tyndale House Publishers, Inc.) 1962.
[4] Bruce, F.F. A Mind for What Matters Collected Essays. (Grand Rapids, MI; Wm. B. Eerdmans Publishing Co, 1990), p 261.

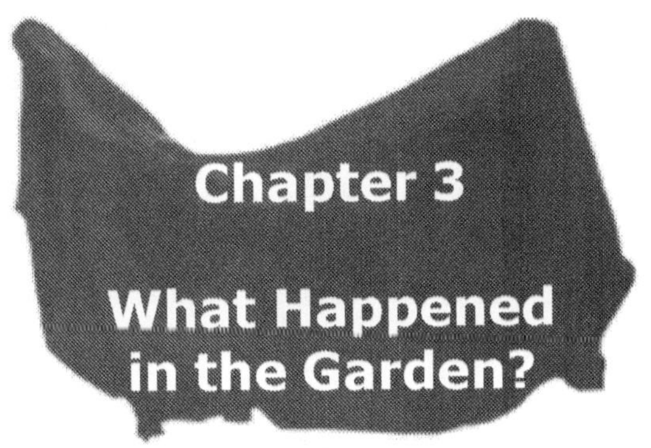

He Made Them Partners

Genesis 1:27-28

So God created man in His *own* image; in the image of God He created him; male and female He created them. Then God blessed them, and God said to them, "Be fruitful and multiply; fill the earth and subdue it; have dominion over the fish of the sea, over the birds of the air, and over **every living thing** that moves on the earth."

God blessed Adam and Eve and commanded them to subdue the earth and have dominion over it. He was not speaking just to Adam. He did not say, "Adam go out and have dominion and Eve you stay here and keep the home fires burning and do whatever Adam tells you". He made them partners. They were to move together in the Spirit of the Lord to subdue the earth, have dominion, push back the enemy's territory, and expand

God's rule on the earth. God made woman, not for man to rule, control, or make decisions for, but to be an equal partner who would rule with him. Sin had not yet corrupted mankind. Strife, aggressiveness, domineering attitudes, lust, and the struggle for preeminence were unknown. "Mankind bore the image and likeness of God Himself. They acted like God, talked like God, loved like God, interacted like God, cared for one another like God, and accepted each other as God accepted them. Where there is the God-kind of love as described by Paul in 1 Corinthians 13, there isn't any desire to take charge of another person."[1]

Robert E. Billings, Jr.'s[2] contention that man has authority over woman because he was created first is nullified by Paul in 1 Cor. 11:12 where he shows that though woman originated from the man, man now has his birth through woman and all come from God. It was sin that brought submission, human authority, rulership, and oppression into the world. Man and woman were to advance the rule of God upon the earth, pushing back the kingdom of darkness and establishing the kingdom of God. There was no separation of these tasks; it was a joint commission and was to be carried out in unity with the Spirit of God.

Sin Changed Everything.

But the fall disrupted that partnership. Sin changed everything.

Genesis 2:8

The Lord God planted a garden eastward in Eden,
and there He put the man whom He had formed.

Genesis 2:15-17

Then the Lord God took the man and put him in
the garden of Eden to tend and keep it. And the
Lord God commanded the man, saying, "Of every
tree of the garden you may freely eat; "but of the
tree of the knowledge of good and evil you shall
not eat, for in the day that you eat of it you shall
surely die."

God planted a beautiful garden, a heavenly headquarters from which the man and woman would expand
God's kingdom on the earth. This would be their home.
Adam was instructed to tend and keep it. The word
tend in the Hebrew is abad {aw-bad^h} which means to
serve, till, work. It also means worshippers. This was a
place where the man and woman would serve God,
worship and commune with Him, and take care of the
garden. God also instructed Adam to *keep* the garden.
This word is shamar {shaw-mar^h} which means to pre-
serve, watch, guard, protect, treasure, be on one's guard,
and to keep closed up. Even Webster's Dictionary defines keep as: to have and hold; to not let go; to maintain; to know a secret and not divulge it; to protect and
defend. Obviously the gate to the garden was not kept
closed as the enemy entered in the guise of a serpent.

Adam's responsibility was to keep the garden pro-
tected and closed off from the enemy. After all, this was
the headquarters, the safe place. When the serpent entered and began the dialogue with Eve, Adam was there
with her (Gen. 3:6). He listened to the dialogue and did

nothing to dissuade Eve, chase out the serpent, or head off the tragedy that ensued. We don't know how long the couple was in the garden before the incident with the serpent. Adam may have gotten complacent or lax in his defense of the garden. But for whatever reason, the enemy came in and began his work of unraveling the safety and security of mankind and their harmony with the Creator.

Eve engaged in conversation with the serpent and just as faith comes by hearing, so doubt was birthed in Eve as she listened to the enemy's reasoning. Was God keeping something good from them, withholding the best of the garden? Why couldn't they eat of this particular tree? Maybe the serpent is right and God doesn't want us to eat because we will become more like Him? As she accepted and believed the lie and ate of the fruit, Adam watched, listened, and did not intervene. Then she handed the fruit to him and he ate as well. But rather than becoming like God, they lost their "God likeness" and became like the serpent — full of self-rule. Losing their covering, the glory of God that kept them close to Him, they attempted to cover themselves. Job says they tried to hide their iniquity, and he charges Adam with initiating the covering:

Job 31:33

> If I have covered my transgressions as Adam, By hiding my iniquity in my bosom,

Now self-aware for the first time, sin changed their very nature and shame drove them to hide behind an inadequate covering that could not alter their condition.

As God came to commune with them, they hid.

Genesis 3:9-12

> Then the L ORD God called to Adam and said to him,
> "Where *are* you?" So he said, "I heard Your voice
> in the garden, and I was afraid because I was na-
> ked; and I hid myself." And He said, "Who told you
> that you *were* naked? Have you eaten from the tree
> of which I commanded you that you should not
> eat?" Then the man said, "The woman whom You
> gave *to be* with me, she gave me of the tree, and I
> ate."

God does not ask questions of us because He needs an answer. Rather He asks questions so that we can recognize where we are. Adam's answer reveals his heart as he blames the woman and God. It had to be God's fault since He was the one who gave the woman to Adam. Adam, after all, never asked for her. He was doing just fine before this creature came along and messed up his idyllic environment. If God had not given him the woman then perhaps he would never have been tempted to eat of the tree. So, in addition to God, Adam blames Eve. She was, after all, the one who handed him the forbidden fruit. He never mentions the conversation with the serpent. In fact, the serpent is never part of Adam's reasoning. Because he only implicates God and Eve, never himself or the serpent, he is indirectly shielding the serpent from any responsibility. This is an act of high treason. Paul tells us clearly that the man entered into this treason with open eyes, knowing exactly what he was doing.

1 Timothy 2:14

> And it was not Adam who was fooled by Satan, but
> Eve, and sin was the result. (The Living Bible)

The division between the genders had begun. Adam looked at Eve as the culprit here and the separation in their relationship widened when God confronted Eve and her response is quite different from his. She had a moment of opportunity to agree with Adam but she chose the path of truth.

Genesis 3:13

> And the LORD God said to the woman, "What *is*
> this you have done?" The woman said, "The ser-
> pent deceived me, and I ate."

Eve answers forthrightly and honestly. Recognizing she has been deceived, she accepts responsibility for her part in this tragedy. Here we are first introduced to "the father of lies" (John 8:44) as Eve implicates the serpent as the one initiating the deception. This candid confession on the part of Eve causes her to be spiritually separated from her husband. She did not back up Adam in his act of treason. Adam and Eve are now not only spiritually separated from God; they are now spiritually separated from each other. There would no longer be partnership between them, but a different dynamic would take its place as a consequence of their actions. God informed them of this new dynamic, not as a curse He was placing on them, but as the result of disobedience. God had set His laws in place, the pillars of the universe, and violation of those laws, physical or spiritual, would bring consequences. Adam and Eve now belonged to Satan and he was master over their fallen nature. They would consequently respond to the earth and each other differently than before.

Genesis 3:17-19

Then to Adam He said, "Because you have heeded the voice of your wife, and have eaten from the tree of which I commanded you, saying, 'You shall not eat of it': "Cursed *is* the ground for your sake; In toil you shall eat *of* it All the days of your life. Both thorns and thistles it shall bring forth for you, And you shall eat the herb of the field. In the sweat of your face you shall eat bread Till you return to the ground, For out of it you were taken; For dust you *are,* And to dust you shall return."

Because of Adam's sin the very earth itself was cursed and it would become laborious for the man to produce fruit. Adam's new, fallen nature, filled with anger and rage, would continue to manifest after their expulsion from the garden. With every new blister, bruise, aching muscle, and failed crop Adam's anger and frustration toward Eve, whom he saw as the cause of all his troubles,[3] would grow into a bitter root of resentment. He would naturally direct those new emotions (borne out of his fallen nature) toward the only other human being — Eve. There is an old saying that "we always hurt the one we love." The ones closest to us inflict the most pain and we cannot know for certain, but Adam may even have become abusive in his frustration over his loss of authority and power. Once he gave up his God given authority to have dominion, the desire to be in control would not have abated because it was his mission in the earth – having dominion over the earth not other human beings. Since it required an outlet, it would naturally have been directed at a new target – the woman.

Misguided Perceptions of Women

This dynamic has plagued mankind since that fateful moment. We find men continuing to blame and punish women for their sins.

September 11, 2001 brought the plight of Muslim women to the forefront of everyone's consciousness. The required clothing for women in that culture reveals the curse of Eve being played out tragically still today. Women must be totally covered or suffer the penalty of law. Why the covering? Women are considered sexual creatures, sirens if you will, who attract men and lead them into sin. In more coarse terms, the idea is that if the woman reveals any part of her anatomy, even her mouth, nose, or lock of hair, the man's lust could be inflamed and he would be tempted to sin. The fault for man's sin lies squarely with this sexual creature whose purpose is procreation. This idea is not strictly Muslim. Charles Trombley in his book, *Who Said Women Can't Teach,* expounds in detail regarding the Jewish law and its perception of women. Founded on a patriarchal system where males always received preference, the Jewish society for many centuries continued to practice polygamy and slavery. In this society women were regarded as property. Women could not receive an education, could not inherit property, could be bought and sold, and were excluded from full participation in religious rites.[4]

And even in the "free world" society we experience in America, the misconceptions of women guide a social order based on, according to Trombley, "fear, prejudice and ignorance with the scales weighted in favor of the male."[5] He validates this opinion with a quote from an article entitled <u>Labels, Assumptions Diminish Women</u> found in the *Tulsa World* on December 5, 1982:

> It showed the bias reflected in our language. Men are termed aggressive, women pushy. Men get annoyed, women hysterical. Single fathers are praiseworthy, single mothers are not. Men assess their lives, women have empty-nest syndrome. Men are ambitious, women clawing. Man's stress is job-related, woman's is due to nerves. An overworked man is a go-getter, an overworked woman disorganized. Men are versatile, women flighty. Older men look distinguished, older women dowdy. The double standard and prejudice are obvious.[6]

God's spoken word to Eve relating the consequences of her actions in the garden continues to be a prophetic reality for women in the earth.

> Genesis 3:16
>
> To the woman He said:
>
> "I will greatly multiply your sorrow and your conception;
> In pain you shall bring forth children;
> Your desire *shall be* for your husband,
> And he shall rule over you."

This scripture is not God cursing Eve, but God telling Eve the consequences of her actions. He had already explained to them what would happen if they ate of the tree in disobedience. He told them they would die. The Hebrew rendering means that "in dying they would die". Once they disobey they die spiritually and consequently begin to die physically. That is the ultimate penalty for sin. Now God is telling Eve what it's going to look like. Some see this as a command of God — that the man was to rule over the woman — that somehow this implies a hierarchical status that now exists between the genders. In fact, this passage of scripture is used most often to prove that women are inferior to men, must not teach men, must be submitted to men, etc. If God ordered such a command, the verb "shall" or "will" depending on your translation would have been in the imperative mood — command. But this verb is in the simple imperfect tense. It translates into English as the future tense. In other words, it is a prophetic statement from God to Eve relating what would happen as a consequence of her sin. He didn't say that men must rule and dominate women, but that they will. If the Hebrew verb were in the imperative mood and a command from God rather than a warning, then the more forcefully a man dominated a woman, the more completely he would fulfill the letter of the law.[7] This reasoning would be laughable if it were not so tragic, for this is how the scripture has been rendered for hundreds of years. A more accurate rendering for this would be "Even though men and marriage will be painful and filled with sorrow, even though your husband will rule you, you'll still desire his company, but he will rule you!" This is not a curse that God put on Eve for disobedience, but a consequence of her actions.

This prophecy has been played out for millennia with few exceptions. Charles Trombley says:

> Even though it was a man who brought sin and death into the world as Paul reiterates so clearly in the book of Romans, it is the women who have suffered the most. By implicating Adam as the originator of sin, he eliminated the grounds for subjugating women as a part of Eve's curse. Doesn't it seem strange, if not contradictory, that man should be exalted to the position of lording it over women when he was the guilty one? However, that is exactly what God said would happen. Not because the Almighty decreed it, but because fallen man would sinfully enforce it.[8]

The rulership of the husband is not a command, but a statement of fact resultant from the sin. If it was indeed a command as some religious scholars profess, then the more a man ruled over, dominated, controlled, and used a woman, the more fully he would be complying with God's law and the more he would please God. What foolishness! If we would just apply common sense, we would see that this scripture couldn't be a command of God. The blood of Jesus Christ on the cross, which was applied to the Mercy Seat, has erased this consequence of sin suffered by women since Eden's tragedy. He bought back the right to subdue the earth and have dominion together by His own death. Men and women have been reinstated into partnership with each other and with God and His original command is not null and void due to sin or passage of time. It stands today as it did in the garden.

Genesis 1:28

> Then God blessed them, and God said to them, "Be fruitful and multiply; fill the earth and subdue it; have dominion over the fish of the sea, over the birds of the air, and over every living thing that moves on the earth."

Since the fall in the garden the woman has looked to the man to meet her needs rather than God from whom she became separated. Men were not created to meet the needs of women and because they try and fail, they respond in frustration, anger, and many other negative ways. Women tend to see men as their spiritual leaders, while men don't really understand fully a woman's needs. The difficulty comes with the instructions in Scripture for men to dwell with their wives with understanding. Because we have misunderstood other Scriptures regarding women, this becomes a challenge.

1 Peter 3:7

> Husbands, likewise, dwell with *them* with **understanding**, giving honor to the wife, as to the weaker vessel, and as *being* **heirs together** of the grace of life, that your prayers may not be hindered.

Yet only God truly knows the heart and only He can fully address the issues of the heart. Ed Silvoso in his book *Women, God's Secret Weapon* says that based on 1 Pet. 3:7 quoted above, men:

> ...must continuously study them and diligently observe them, not to invalidate or change what they do not comprehend, but to accept women the way they are.[9]

He also says:

> If men were to study the contour of a
> woman's soul with the same interest with
> which they scrutinize the shape of her body,
> there would be little misunderstanding be-
> tween the sexes. Unfortunately, ignorance
> of what is inside a woman provides a life-
> line for the bigotry that characterizes so
> many prejudicial responses to female ac-
> tions and behavior.[10]

The Promise of a Seed

With the dire prophecy spoken over the woman
in Genesis 3:16, however, God promised a blessing — a
time when the seed of the woman would bruise the head
of the serpent, would strip him of his authority in the
earth.

1 John 3:8

> The one who practices sin is of the devil; for the
> devil has sinned from the beginning. The Son of
> God appeared for this purpose, that He might de-
> stroy the works of the devil.

Church traditions have continued to preach the
curse rather than the Cross. What happened in the garden was a work of the devil, wholly and completely. Jesus
destroyed the work of the devil and is continuing to destroy his work through all those who believe on His name
— men and women. He conquered Satan, restoring
mankind to the original oneness they shared in the garden before the fall, removing the curse of sin. The authority to subdue the earth and have dominion was given

totally to Jesus Christ and He passed it on to us. All the struggles of subjugation, taking charge, bossiness, rebellion, etc. were removed because they are sin. Christ opened up a new and living way and together we are reunited with God in perfect union and harmony.

As we walk in the spirit and not in the flesh, we begin to subdue the earth. Our walk becomes fruitful in that we multiply. More and more are brought out of the kingdom of darkness and translated into the Kingdom of God. We must put our corrupt, selfish humanity and the subsequent consequences of that fallen nature on the altar of sacrifice. Laying down the need to dominate, rule, control, subdue, and exclude each other from major leadership roles, we can pick up God's mantle and begin to rule over and subdue the earth. Only when men and women work together, as partners, can we begin to fulfill God's purposes in the earth.

God did not just reveal His perfect plan for women in the Garden of Eden; He continued to demonstrate the cherished place of women in His heart throughout scripture. In the next chapter we shall look at one story in the Old Testament where God demonstrates his intent for men and women to join together in unity and harmony. In that place He would open the wells of revival.

Chapter Three Notes

[1] Trombley, Charles. *Who Said Women Can't Teach?* (South Plainfield, NJ: Bridge Publlishing, Inc., 1985). p 74.

[2] Billings, Robert E. Jr. "Should Women Speak in the Church." (1 Aug. 2000): p 7. Online. Internet 13 May 2001.

[3] Adam blamed God and the woman: Genesis 3:12

[4] Trombley. p 26.

[5] IBID. p 82.

[6] IBID. p 82.

[7] IBID. p 112-113.

[8] IBID. p 114

[9] Silvoso, Ed. "Women, God's Secret Weapon." (Ventura, CA: Regal Books, 2001). p 98.

[10] IBID. p 97.

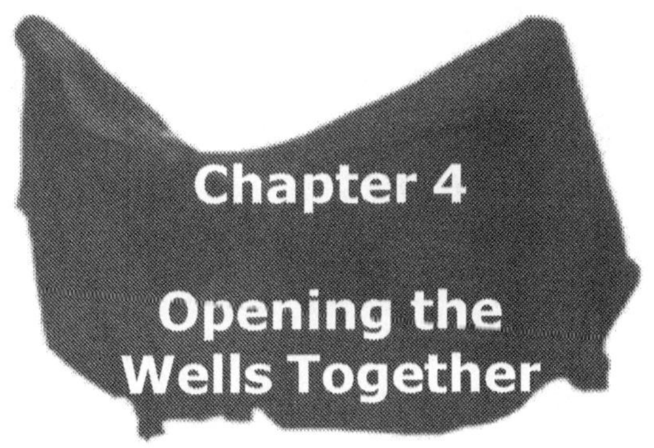

God Speaks to the Hearts of Women

Acts 2:17

And it shall come to pass in the last days, God declares, that I will pour out of My Spirit upon all mankind, and your sons and your daughters shall prophesy telling forth the divine counsels] and your young men shall see visions (divinely granted appearances), and your old men shall dream divinely suggested] dreams. (Amplified)

The Spirit of the Lord has been moving on the hearts of women over the last 150 years — more so, it seems, than any time in history. Why? Perhaps, as many of the prophets are saying, we are truly in the last days. Azusa Street can be traced back to the first few years of the last century when revival began breaking out in many places around the country and even to a young woman, Agnes Ozman, who received her prayer language at a remote school in Kansas City, half way across the country from Azusa Street. That language has reverberated around the world and continues to echo today.

Women have been more vocal about their "inherent" rights in the last two centuries and their voices have been raised around the world virtually simultaneously. The United States of America was founded on the principle of "religious freedom". It was God ordained and it appeared His blessing was on our country as He poured Himself into the lives of people as this democracy was established. Because men of God, hungry after God, began the work here, and because this was a country where religious freedom was touted as a basic foundation, all people began to sense in their hearts that desire for freedom to be manifest.

Luke 6:45

A good man out of the good treasure of his heart brings forth good; and an evil man out of the evil treasure of his heart brings forth evil. For out of the abundance of the heart his mouth speaks.

The heart cry for all people in the colonies was for freedom to worship God, seek God, rule themselves under the authority of God, and to express that freedom in a unique and independent way. When the heart desire of a people is suppressed in any way, there is usually an overreaction to the inhibition of the expression of that freedom. The women were not offered the same freedoms. In fact, because of the consequences of Eve's action in the Garden, women were still subjected to the whims of selfish and prideful men who thought for the most part that women were like children

— they were to be seen but not heard. Consequently, women rose up to express the same heart's desire that had formed this country under God. The "Suffragettes", "Women's Liberation", and other similar movements were in response to the moving of God's Spirit upon the hearts of women to stand up and take their place beside the men, for together they would woo and win the heart of God, and His Spirit would come in power bringing revival to the nation. The problem came when the scales of justice tilted out of balance. As God was calling to women, that call was going out across the earth and women, saved or not, were hearing the call.

In Nations that claim a democracy, women began to win the right to vote just in the last 110 years. New Zealand in 1893; Australia in 1902; Finland in 1906; Norway in 1913. In 1920, the United States gave women full equal voting rights and in 1928 women from the age of 21 received equal voting rights with men in England. Between 1914 and 1939 women achieved this right in 28 additional countries. After World War II other countries joined the group including France, Italy, Romania, Yugoslavia, China, India, and Pakistan.[1] This movement was for the most part contained within the last one hundred and fifty years.

Then came the Women's Liberation movement. A lot of good came out of this movement, but there was also a lot of alienation that occurred because of the way women went about establishing their independence. Women were never meant to be independent, but designed by God to be totally dependent on the Spirit of God and co-dependent with men to achieve the purposes of God on the earth. The women's liberation movement caused the pendulum to swing so far left that Gay Rights was birthed as an alternative lifestyle, men were seen as unnecessary and irrelevant, and some of the more radical women advocated treating men in the same way they had been treated for centuries. It was a knee jerk, retaliatory, vengeful motivation. But even though we live in a fallen world and these particular aggressive initiatives by women have caused alienation and birthed new issues in society, they still served to bring women's issues to the attention of the world. These movements have done much to afford women equality in status and pay in the workplace, a voice in the workings of government, and fairer treatment in much of society. But the consequences of Adam and Eve's disobedience are still seen in the earth.

As we begin, however, to get the revelation of God's true plan for all of us and the fact that Jesus' death rent the veil of separation between us and God and between us and each other we are finally beginning to move together in a desire for more of God, regardless of age, sex, race, culture, denomination, or theological understanding. Most of the church has accepted the reconciliation of God and humanity, but they have been slow to accept the other aspects of redemption, i.e. equality, power, authority, and dominion over the powers of darkness. Prejudices, domination, control, and ungodly rulership, still abound in the earth.

Unfortunately there are many women who agree with the prejudices of church tradition. I always found this difficult to accept until I realized that some of us choose to live by the accepted interpretations because it allows us to put the responsibility for our spiritual maturity on the male figures in our lives. We can always say, "It is my husband's, my pastor's responsibility to 'cover' me and ensure that I grow in Christ. It's the man's job"! Again this goes back to Eden where God warned Eve that her desire would be for her husband. Many women see men as their spiritual head and, therefore, responsible for their spiritual growth and maturity. The revealing truth, however, is that on judgment day when we stand before our God, the men in our lives will not be standing with us. We stand naked and alone before the one with whom we have to do (Heb. 4:13), and alone we answer for our lives. We must take responsibility to answer the call of God on our lives and obey Him rather than man (Acts 4:19). If it goes against tradition, are we willing to make the sacrifice and accept persecution for the Word's sake? We don't exert authority for the sake of pushing ourselves forward. We quietly obey God for obedience is all He requires of us.[2] When there is a conflict, we must follow after peace. Peace in God does not always mean peace with man. Our hearts convict us of the truth. Jesus brought division, a sword, and He expects us to answer to Him for our actions.

God's Plan Born in Humility

God's plan for mankind was established in the Garden of Eden and His plans and purposes will be fulfilled in the earth. This coming revival will be born in humble and surprising places. Revival comes first in embryonic form, just as Jesus came as a baby born in a stable. It took revelation from God for anyone to know He had arrived and so only people of faith will see that what is happening now is just an infant and it will grow up to be something bigger.

Just as Elizabeth spoke to Mary about her being the mother of her Lord - speaking from faith.

Just as Simeon and Anna at the temple saw with the eyes of faith the savior of their people in the infant Jesus.

For this revival to be birthed into fullness, it will take men and women of faith moving together in the will of God. Just as Jesus was met at the temple by a man and a woman who both prayed over and prophesied over Him, Simeon and Anna (Luke 2:27-), so too the ear mark of this revival will be that both male and female together will bring forth what He is purposing in these last days. We are now experiencing renewal. In some places it is happening corporately but mostly it occurs in the hearts of individuals as the Lord creates in them a clean heart along with a passion for His presence. As people begin to walk in holiness and come together to seek His face, He will begin to pour out His power and we will see the dead raised, the lame walking, the deaf ears hearing, the lost saved — not just in a trickle but in a torrent.

The revival will be characterized by unity in the body, male and female, young and old, Jew and Gentile, — a corporate army empowered, united, and working together in a spirit of collaboration in order to accomplish the mission God has set before us. This will prepare us for the final days' end time harvest.

Jesus came to set the captives free. Women in the church have been held captive, but the truth of Jesus' liberating birth, death, and resurrection has come and the truth sets women free. Women have been held back and disqualified from the public ministry of the Lord Jesus Christ and now is the time when God is freeing the captives, removing the restraints, and bringing women into the Promised Land. In her book "*Women of Destiny*", Cindy Jacobs writes:

> Of one thing I am certain: *God is calling women today in a greater way than He ever has before.* Major prophetic voices are prophesying all around the world that this is the time to find a way to release women into the ministry. The different prophesies say things such as, 'God is raising up a new generation of women ministers in the anointing of an Esther or Deborah.' Others announce, 'Make way for the women, for God is pouring out His end-time anointing on His handmaidens.'[3]

A Story in Genesis

In Genesis Chapter 28 we read the story of Isaac blessing his sons. Jacob was sent away by his father to find a wife among his own kin. He left his home, his mother, brother, friends, all that was familiar and headed out to his uncle's land. He spent the night in a certain place and there God visited him.

Genesis 28:12-17

12 Then he dreamed, and behold, a ladder *was* set up on the earth, and its top reached to heaven; and there the angels of God were ascending and descending on it.13 And behold, the LORD stood above it and said: "I *am* the LORD God of Abraham

your father and the God of Isaac; the land on which you lie I will give to you and your descendants.14 "Also your descendants shall be as the dust of the earth; you shall spread abroad to the west and the east, to the north and the south; and in you and in your seed all the families of the earth shall be blessed.15 "Behold, I *am* with you and will keep you wherever you go, and will bring you back to this land; for I will not leave you until I have done what I have spoken to you."16 Then Jacob awoke from his sleep and said, "Surely the LORD is in this place, and I did not know *it*."17 And he was afraid and said, "How awesome *is* this place! This *is* none other than the house of God, and this *is* the gate of heaven!"

Leaving the ones you love to journey into a strange land alone, without friends or family, is not pleasant for anyone so it would be logical to assume that Jacob set out on this journey with heavy heart. But along the way God reestablishes His covenant with Abraham, Isaac, and now Jacob. He promises to be with Jacob always and at some point to bring him back to his own land. The morning after his encouraging dream, Jacob continues his journey with a different attitude.

Genesis 28:20-29:1

20 Then Jacob made a vow, saying, "If God will be with me, and keep me in this way that I am going, and give me bread to eat and clothing to put on,21 "so that I come back to my father's house in peace, then the LORD shall be my God.22 "And this stone which I have set as a pillar shall be God's house, and of all that You give me I will surely give a tenth

to You." So Jacob went on his journey and came to the land of the people of the East.

The phrase "went on" comes from the Hebrew word nasa' { **naw-saw'**} which means to lift up, be exalted, be carried away. Jacob literally was lifting up his feet, kicking up his heels, joyously continuing his journey with a light heart knowing that he was about to encounter his destiny. It is with this new vision and awakened heart that he comes into the land of his uncle, Laban.

Genesis 29:2-3

And he looked, and saw a well in the field; and behold, there *were* three flocks of sheep lying by it; for out of that well they watered the flocks. A large stone *was* on the well's mouth.3 Now all the flocks would be gathered there; and they would roll the stone from the well's mouth, water the sheep, and put the stone back in its place on the well's mouth.

According to Kevin J. Conner's book, *Interpreting The Symbols and Types,* a well is a symbol of refreshment, a source of water of life.[4] A well oftentimes refers to the blessings of God. We often talk about redigging the wells of revival, or drinking at the well. In John 4, Jesus at the well talked about living water, and a well of water springing up to everlasting life. Jesus referred to himself as the giver of living water (John 4:10). He is the well from which we drink. Churches everywhere are praying for the "wells" of revival to be open that all may come and drink.

Revelation 21:6

> And He said to me, "It is done! I am the Alpha and the Omega, the Beginning and the End. I will give of the fountain of the water of life freely to him who thirsts.

So Jacob comes to a well where the sheep are gathered but none are drinking and there is a stone over the well's mouth. According to Ira Milligan in his book *Understanding The Dreams You Dream,* a stone can be a "Witness: word, testimony, person, precept, accusations, persecution".[5] And finally we find there are three shepherds ("brothers" Gen. 29:4) with their flocks. In the study of numbers there are both positive and negative connotations. Ira Milligan defines the number three as "Conform: Obey, copy, imitate, likeness, **tradition**".[6] (Emphasis mine). What does all this mean — a well, a stone covering the well, and three flocks around the well but not drinking?

Jacob arrives at this location, takes in the scene and makes a very logical suggestion, but receives a strange answer.

Genesis 29:7-8

> Then he said, "Look, *it is* still high day; *it is* not time for the cattle to be gathered together. Water the sheep, and go and feed *them.*" But they said, "We cannot until all the flocks are gathered together, and they have rolled the stone from the well's mouth; then we water the sheep."

The three shepherds answer that they *cannot* remove the stone from the well. Obviously three burly shepherds have the physical strength necessary to remove the stone, so it is not their physical inability that restrains them. They are restrained from removing the stone from the well and watering their flocks because they are *not permitted* to do so until all the flocks are gathered. They must wait for the rest of the flocks.

What is keeping the stone over our wells of revival? It was a **large stone** covering the well's mouth — an obstruction covering the blessing of God, the place of watering, and the living water. There are many suggestions argued in the body of Christ regarding what it takes to bring true revival. Some argue for reconciliation with Native Americans, unity in the body, mothering and fathering the next generation, ministering to the poor, and removing sin from the camp. One additional witness that could be added to the list that is stopping the flow of living water is the traditions of the church that choose not to receive the female shepherdess' and their flocks. These issues in and of themselves do not cause revival nor can anyone singly prevent it; revival is a gift from our Beloved which can be sustained through our obedience. These issues, rather than bringing revival, begin to be healed as the Spirit of God pours out on all flesh and touches the woundedness in our souls. In order for the healing to begin, however, we must first recognize that we have a problem, a wound that needs mending. When we accept the fact that our traditions have kept the stone over the well, acknowledge that we may be missing revelation, and ask His help in knowing truth, He will remove the stone (traditions) and healing will begin, bridges will be built, and we will all begin to experience a dimension of His Glory as yet untouched.

Jesus rebukes the Pharisees for adhering to their unholy traditions and reminds them that only their traditions can usurp the power of the Word of God.

> Matthew 15:6
>
> Thus you have made the commandment of God of no effect by your tradition.
>
> The New American Standard says it like this:
>
> Matthew 15:6
>
> And *thus* you invalidated the word of God for the sake of your tradition.

The word of God is the most powerful force in the universe. By it He upholds all things:

> Hebrews 1:3
>
> ...who being the brightness of *His* glory and the express image of His person, and upholding all things by the **word of His power**, when He had by Himself purged our sins, sat down at the right hand of the Majesty on high...

And yet Jesus declares that we have the power to invalidate the word of God making it ineffective. That is an incredible statement, but Jesus gave to mankind the authority to speak His word. What we speak has power and when our declarations line up with the word of God, God confirms that word with signs following. But when our declarations are from head knowledge, by rote, or by tradition, no power is released. We cause the word to be ineffective by our traditions that lack the real time revelation of the truth of God.

The surprising revelation in this story of Jacob and Rachel comes in the next verse:

Genesis 29:9-11

Now while he was still speaking with them, Rachel came with her father's sheep, for she was a shepherdess. And it came to pass, when Jacob saw Rachel the daughter of Laban his mother's brother, and the sheep of Laban his mother's brother, that Jacob went near and rolled the stone from the well's mouth, and watered the flock of Laban his mother's brother. Then Jacob kissed Rachel, and lifted up his voice and wept.

When Rachel, the shepherdess, arrives with her *father's* sheep, Jacob immediately comes to her aid and removes the stone (traditions of men) that kept the sheep from being watered. As a type and shadow of our redeemer and the one who gives us living water, Jacob came to the aid of his beloved. He had just been given the assurance from God that all the peoples of the earth would be blessed through his seed.[7] His heart rejoiced when he saw Rachel for he was seeing with the eyes of faith. He had just had a visitation of God, a dream full of promise, and he was still filled with the glory of the vision when she appeared. She was a shepherdess, probably smelly, dirty, sunburned, and unkempt. But Jacob looked past the physical and saw the promise of the Father in her. He kissed her and wept with joy. What an incredible picture of our Beloved! Rachel definitely represents in this story the women that are to be included in public ministry, but she also represents the church. Our Beloved is waiting for the church to arrive at the revelation that all the issues we are facing must at least be addressed if not totally resolved.

A further type of our redeemer is revealed in Moses when in one small Scripture, easily overlooked, he too comes to the aid of the shepherdess.

> Exodus 2:16-17
>
> Now a priest of Midian had seven daughters, and they came to draw water and fill the troughs to water their father's flock. Some shepherds came along and drove them away, but Moses got up and came to their rescue and watered their flock. (NIV)

To Pastor or Not to Pastor

Jesus is the one who will remove the stone that covers the well of revival. It is with unabashed joy that He removes the stone and pours out the living water (Heb. 12:2).

The word Pastor is used only one time in the New Testament. This term and the meaning of the office have been elevated by tradition to a status that it was never meant to have. Nowhere in the Bible does it say that women cannot be pastors. And even those persons who attempt to be more fair-minded and allow women the role of associate pastors say they still cannot be senior pastors. There is no scriptural basis to back up this opinion. It is merely a tradition held over from a patriarchal society that Jesus (as well as Paul) came strongly against in His teachings.

God gave the five-fold ministry to the church and there is no gender differentiation attributed to any of the gifts – a pastor is a shepherd or shepherdess.

Ephesians 4:11-12

And He Himself gave some *to be* apostles, some prophets, some evangelists, and some pastors and teachers, for the equipping of the saints for the work of ministry, for the edifying of the body of Christ,

These five gifts relate to each other horizontally with no established hierarchy, and all submit to Christ the head. This does not preclude leadership in the body. But the place of leadership belongs to the mature in Christ for in maturity there is no desire for elevated position. Jesus is looking for a servant's heart in church leadership, not someone who will use, abuse, or revel in a position. There is a structure established by God and it is God who places people into position of leadership. And as Jesus said:

Mark 10:43

Yet it shall not be so among you; but whoever desires to become great among you shall be your servant.

No One Can Do It Alone

Just as importantly as the three shepherds not being permitted to remove the stone, however, is the fact that Rachel could not have removed the stone by herself. She would have needed the help and support of the men. But even when she arrived, they had no need to remove the stone; Jacob did that for them, sovereignly. When God sends revival, when He removes the stone, both genders must recognize that God created us to partner together to produce fruit.

We have held to our traditions for far too long and the world has not been saved. We must examine the way we have been doing business as a body. The United States has sent more missionaries out to foreign lands than any other country and yet our own country is becoming more and more depraved and sin-ridden. As the church has turned a complacent eye to the laws being passed allowing the abominations of sin to rule our society, our country has begun to be ruled more and more by the enemy of God. And yet we continue to hold tenaciously to our traditions, which cause the Word of God to be powerless and ineffectual.

Matthew 15:6

So for the sake of your tradition (the rules handed down by your forefathers), you have set aside the Word of God [depriving it of force and authority and making it of no effect]. (Amplified Bible)

Let us set aside the traditions that have kept women in bondage and take up the sword of the Spirit, the Word of God, and let men and women together seek His hand to open the wells of revival. It will take all of us working together, preaching, teaching, evangelizing, healing the sick, raising the dead, cleansing the lepers, and in all places proclaiming the good news for the world to be won for Christ.

Yes, I included teaching. Space does not permit that all the "controversial" scriptures be covered in this book. But we shall look at one and examine thoroughly the subject of whether women can teach.

Chapter Four Notes

[1] This is a compilation of data from dozens of on-line information sources. A key word search for "women's right to vote" will yield a plethora of data.

[2] One of the most common things we pray against in Christians is the "fear of man" (Proverbs 29:25). We are concerned what others might think, or how we might be perceived. For men, there is no excuse; but for women, we have used men as our excuse not to obey God. We could excuse ourselves because tradition would not allow us; we could tell the men what we thought God was saying and they could follow through; or we could just say we are prohibited from speaking and God understands. Jesus, by His death, removed all excuses.

[3] Jacobs, Cindy. *Women of Destiny*. (Ventura, Calif.: Regal Books, 1998) p. 173.

[4] Conner, Kevin J. *Interpreting Symbols and Types*. .Revised and Expanded Edition (Portland, Oregon: City Bible Publishing, 1992). p.179.

[5] Milligan, Ira. *Understanding The Dreams You Dream*. (Shippensburg, PA. Destiny Image Publishers, Inc. 1997) Third Printing. p 224.

[6] IBID. p 92.

[7] Even though the tribe of Judah did not come through Rachel, she had two sons -- Joseph meaning, "Jehovah has added", and Benjamin meaning "Son of the right hand" or "anointing". Joseph had two sons, Manasseh meaning, "God has made me forget all my trouble", and Ephraim meaning "God has made me fruitful in the land of my afflictions". These sons all prophetically point to the ministry of women in the end time church. Women are as much anointed, sons of the right hand, as are men, and women will bring freedom, deliverance, and provision to the corporate body as they are released into ministry.

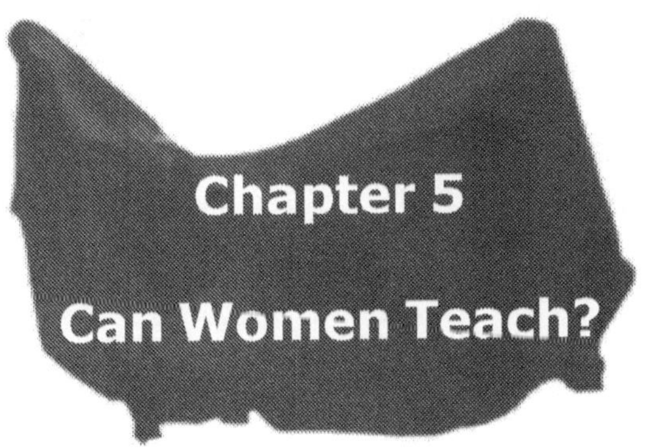

I wish to open this chapter with an excerpt from an article written by Dr. Gregory Boyd, theologian and teacher, which exemplifies the struggle many women engage in when sensing a call from God to teach.

Kathy's struggle with temptation.

Kathy was one of the brightest students I've ever had in my theology courses. She asked insightful questions and often contributed to lively class discussions. The time and energy she put into her theology classes was motivated by more than just a desire to get a good grade – she was passionately interested in the material.

I became concerned when Kathy began to withdraw in class. She held back and seemed to second-guess herself when she did join in discussions. So when she stopped me in the cafeteria one afternoon and said, "I really feel like I've been under attack since I started studying theology," I was anxious to hear what she had to say, but was grieved when I learned the reason behind her struggle.

It went something like this, "Here's the problem – I'm really struggling with temptation. Whenever I think about the future, I see myself in ministry in the church, preaching the gospel. I can't think of anything I'd rather do and I can't get this idea out of my head. Why is God letting the devil torment me with something I can never do?"

I asked her why she felt like it would be wrong for her to preach the gospel. "Well, I always picture it in the context of a large group of people, like in front of a church." She explained that in her church tradition, women were not allowed to minister in leadership positions or have authority over men. They believed the Bible said that some spiritual gifts and ministry positions – such as preaching or teaching – were for men only.[1]

The model for church that we see today, a building or structure where one man is pastor, and on Sunday morning people congregate to sing a few songs, have announcements, hear a message from the man of God, and perhaps have some prayer time has no basis in Scripture. The writer of Hebrews precludes the model of church that resurrected the Levitical priesthood (one ex. Heb. 7:11) allowing only one man to approach God for the remission of our sins, along with all its rites, rituals, pomp, and legalism. Elizabeth Tetlow states it this way:

In the first century, the Church was in the process of working out its understanding, theology and structures of ministry, and there is no scriptural evidence that the model of a Levitical priesthood was ever introduced. In the Old Testament the Levitical model had developed connotations of power and status, sexism and hierarchy. When it was finally introduced into Christianity in the second through the fourth centuries, hierarchical status, power, and the exclusion of women from official ministry appeared at the same time.[2]

Jesus fulfilled all the Old Testament requirements and wiped out the handwriting of the law becoming the last high priest for all eternity. His church was birthed on Calvary and was nurtured and grew in homes where a handful, perhaps as many as 25 or more gathered together to talk about, learn about, and worship the Lord. Women were in these homes. If, as tradition tells us (based on interpretation of 1 Timothy 2:11), women are not to speak or teach, then they have been apparently violating the Word of God throughout the centuries. If women are not to teach then why have they written books, taught Bible studies, taught individuals about our resurrected Savior, gone to foreign lands to work on the mission field, and in all other ways "taught" the Word of God? If this were exclusively for men only, then everything women do that falls under the category of "teaching" would be a violation of God's word.

Theologian Gregory Boyd says that:

In the ancient world, boys over the age of thirteen were considered men. So if this passage (1 Timothy 2:11) is taken literally and applied today as it was applied in the first century, it would exclude women from serving as Sunday school teachers, youth leaders, worship leaders, or missionaries for boys over the age of thirteen.[3]

Dr. Boyd goes on to say that:

Paul doesn't say that women shouldn't have authority over men in their own culture, he just says, "over a man." That would mean that a woman under any circumstances, in any condition, in any culture, should not have authority over any man. But even the Catholic Church throughout its history and certainly the Protestant church, has permitted women to minister in the mission field. In other words, it's okay to have authority over Chinese men, and over African men, and over Russian men, as long as women don't have authority over men of their own culture.[4]

Dr. Boyd agrees in his article that this notion is foolish and it certainly seems so when viewed from this learned perspective and from the rest of Paul's teachings such as when he instructs Titus:

Titus 2:3

Bid the older women...to give good counsel *and* be **teachers** of what is right *and* noble...

Is there truly a contradiction in Scripture or does this passage really mean that women are not to teach unless they are "older" and then only under certain circumstances? We know there is no contradiction in Scripture because God inspired all Scripture and He makes no mistakes.

All Scripture must be viewed in the light of the redemption of Jesus Christ. If we looked at Scripture through the blood of Christ and the Cross of Calvary, we would see God's plan for all of mankind – freedom, power, authority, unity, victory, equality, and an eternity of ruling and reigning together with Him. As stated in Chapter 2, we have accepted the curse that came as a consequence of sin, not the Cross that redeemed us from those consequences as doctrine, and women have been enslaved by this erroneous prohibition to teach. It has even been said that if a woman was anointed to teach, then her anointing must have come from Satan because Scripture prohibits her teaching and, therefore, God would not anoint her. Cindy Jacobs says:

> There are times when we have to look around and say, "If God is using women in such powerful ways in the Church, maybe we need to reevaluate our thinking, *for they are either tools of the devil, or blessed by God* to fulfill a place that I didn't think they could in my paradigm."[5]

The Holy Spirit was given to transform us into the image of Christ. As we are transformed we begin to emulate Him and we take from His ministry our examples on how to function in the kingdom. Jesus was a servant embodying all the ascension gifts — evangelist, teacher, apostle, prophet, and pastor. All the gifts are to serve mankind for the glory of God. In the New Testament these gifts all served the people of God, each with his or her own gifts, for the building up of the Christian community in love. They never were to rule over, lord over, or have authority over the body of Christ. Jesus alone is the head. The body is for service. No distinction was ever made in Jesus' ministry between men and women. In fact, He honored women as much as the men. The woman at the well (John 4), Mary at the tomb (John 20), the women at Simon's house (Luke 7), and other women Jesus encountered were all given honor, love, and respect. Jesus used each situation to demonstrate that women and men are equal in His eyes. He continued to break tradition in almost every encounter with a woman and it caused his disciples no small amount of confusion (example John 4:27).

Acts 11:26 tells us that Jesus' disciples were first called Christians in Antioch. The word "Christian" literally means, "little anointed." These people were not only following Christ's example, complying with His teaching, and performing miracle signs and wonders, they were acting like the Master. This is authentic Christianity; that which most totally conforms to the nature of Jesus' own ministry. His ministry was that of service to all humanity, regardless of class, gender, or merit. It was demonstrated by atoning, self-offering love.

The later exclusion of women from official church ministry raises serious questions about the authenticity of such a practice. New Testament evidence demonstrated that the exclusion of women from ministry is neither in accord with the teaching or practice of Jesus nor with that of the first century church. Jesus' call to discipleship and to ministerial service were universal. Frank

Viola, in his open letter concerning a woman's role in the church, defines the message given by restricting women.

> I had to ask myself a telling question. 'What clear message is sent by silencing the sisters in the church meetings? Supposing that God originated this idea, what message is He conveying through such a mandate?' The answer is as arresting as it is alarming. The undeniable message is that men cannot learn anything from women. Nor can they be ministered to spiritually by a woman![6]

Since women as well as men can be filled with the Spirit of God (Acts 2:4), it would seem contrary to the purposes of God to forbid women to share with others, anywhere, anytime, in any setting.

1 Timothy 2:11-14

Based on the above arguments, we must examine 1 Timothy 2:11-14 fully.

1 Timothy 2:11-14

> Let a woman learn in silence with all submission. And I do not permit a woman to teach or to have authority over a man, but to be in silence. For Adam was formed first, then Eve. And Adam was not deceived, but the woman being deceived, fell into transgression.

If this Scripture doesn't really mean that women are not to teach, what does it mean? The church has established an entire doctrine and practice on this one portion of text. This is unprecedented. It is a generally accepted practice that at least three corroborating scriptures are needed to form a doctrine or practice. But with this one text, doctrine was formed. In these last days a wealth of information is beginning to be revealed showing that this one portion of text (as in the case of many others) has been misunderstood, mistranslated, and misinterpreted. To correctly understand any Scripture we must apply the rules of interpretation. All Scripture is God-breathed and, therefore, alive with revelation. The Spirit of God must teach us the true application of any Scripture – in the past when it was written, in the present for now application, and prophetically in the future. We must look at the words based on definition, usage, culture, context, historical background, precedent, and logic.

For the most part, the translators ignored the social situation, the cultural context of this letter. Paul was writing to Timothy in Ephesus. This is crucial to understanding Paul's intent in this passage. Ephesus was the world center of paganism at that time, believed by the people to be ruled by a mother goddess named Artemus. It was famous for its shrine of Diana which the Romans called Artemus, where thousands of prostitutes believed fornication brought believers into contact with deity.

The key elements of this pagan culture were 1) the worship of a female diety, 2) the teaching of female superiority and domination over men, 3) and a teaching of feminine procreation — the belief that this goddess could bring forth offspring without the help of a male. The cult was characterized by sexual perversion, fertility rites, myths, and elaborate geneologies where people would trace their lineage through their mother's line rather than through the father's. Magic and demonic activity enforced these erroneous beliefs.

When women immersed in this pagan culture received Christ, as new Christian converts, they had to unlearn their pagan practices. Until they received Scriptural teaching that changed their worldview, they continued to put forth their erroneous doctrines based on myths and fables, believing they possessed a special kind of hidden knowledge. And because of their belief in acquiring divine union through fornication, their teaching often included an offering of sexual favors to complete the transition to godliness.

There was, also, a large contingent of Jewish Gnostics that had settled in Ephesus. Gnosticism was the 1st century equivalent of the New Age movement. These Gnostics began mixing the teachings of Artemus with the doctrines of demons. They had their own spirit guides who taught them and they mixed the teachings of Artemus and the doctrines of their spirit guides, with the teachings of the Old Testament. One belief that meshed well with the Artemus cult was about Adam, Eve, and the serpent in the Garden. The most consistent version of this story in Gnosticism is that the Hebrew God, whose name they changed from YAHWEH to bealdebaals, made a mistake in creating the physical universe, because all matter is evil to a Gnostic and only what is spiritual is good. According to their misunderstanding, the creator god is inferior to the serpent who becomes the savior of mankind. This is the basis of Luciferian doctrine on which many cults, including Freemasonry, is based. The serpent becomes the revealer of truth who brings true knowledge. The Greek word for knowledge is "gnosis" from which we derive Gnosticism. In the story Eve is the illuminator because she is the first to receive this true knowledge from the serpent and she becomes the teacher of this new revelation to Adam.

This Gnostic cult came into the church, beginning to infiltrate and to teach that Eve, being the mother of all, was the progenitor (founder, originator) of humanity and that Adam came later from Eve and was in fact not her husband but her son. So here we have Eve as the recipient of special revelation and the originator of the human race. The word "originator" is in the Greek "authenteo" which we will discuss in a moment.

Timothy, the young pastor left in Ephesus to help mature the work there, had a mess on his hands. Paul is telling Timothy what he needs to do about this heretical problem. In his letter to Timothy, Paul expounds on how the church is to conduct itself as a people of God; but he was mainly encouraging and authorizing Timothy to preach against false teachers and their doctrines. The entire letter is soaked with this theme, beginning and ending with instructions to halt the spread of false doctrines. Starting right from the first verse in his letter to Timothy, Paul writes:

> 1 Timothy 1:3
>
> As I urged you when I was on my way to Macedonia, stay on where you are at Ephesus in order that you may warn *and* admonish *and* charge certain individuals not to teach any different doctrine, (Amplified Bible)

and ending with:

1 Timothy 6:20

O Timothy, guard *and* keep the deposit entrusted [to you]! Turn away from the irreverent babble *and* godless chatter, with the vain *and* empty *and* worldly phrases, and the subtleties *and* the con-tradictions in what is falsely called knowledge *and* spiritual illumination.

Paul instructs Timothy to oppose false teaching. Oppose those who utter blasphemy against the living God, which means to speak things about God that are not true. He says avoid myths, avoid endless genealo-gies, warn people about the doctrine of demons, have nothing to do with old wives tales. And the most wide-spread wives' tale was the one about Eve, Adam, and the serpent. Paul says to have nothing to do with stu-pid, senseless controversy. On the other hand he says to give sound teaching, use the Scriptures for they are profitable for teaching, reproof, for training in all righ-teousness. He says to rightly divide the word of truth.

Here is Paul, trained in the oral law, the written law, and the most religious of men, who knew that un-der Jewish law a woman was not allowed to learn the Torah. And yet, after his conversion, he comes aggres-sively against the traditions of men that have been passed down by the oral law.

1 Timothy 2:11

"Let a woman learn..."

He begins with his main point in verse 11 "let a woman learn": This sentiment is diametrically opposed to Jewish custom where women were often excluded from the learning process. Paul, however, understood the necessity of them learning and teaching sound doctrine. Why? "Because their lack of pure Biblical knowledge was causing confusion and their zeal had to be harnessed."[7] And not only were they causing confusion, but in 2 Timothy, Chapter 3, he noted that Ephesian women were being led astray by false teachers and in 1 Tim. 5:15 he decried that some were turning away and following Satan. These women had little knowledge of Scripture; they were new Christians, converted Gnostics, full of false doctrine and heresies. Paul wanted them to learn, but in quietness, submitting to the authority of scripture, not teaching or arguing for their false doctrine. The popular question-and-answer format was used both in pagan philosophical and church teaching during this time period. There were heated debates as ideas were tossed around and confusion piled upon confusion. In 1 Tim. 1:4 and 6:20, Paul tells us there were endless discussions and quibbling over the meaning and interpretation of words.

1 Timothy 2:11

"Let a woman learn in silence with all submission".

In the last part of this sentence, Paul says women are to learn in "silence", and learn in a proper manner. The word translated "silence" is **"hesuchia" (hay-soo-khee'-ah)** more correctly translated "in humble quietness". It also means harmony, peace, conformity or agreement. Paul says she must be in agreement – that is in agreement with the scriptures, in agreement with sound teaching, in agreement with the church.

This is the same Greek word used in 1 Timothy 2:2 when he said he wanted the church to pray for governmental leaders so that we may live a peaceful (hesuchia) life. He was not advocating silence, but peace. Quietness was a life free from arguments, stress and turmoil. He was basically saying, "Women, sit down and learn with respect and quietness. Be reverent and learn."

In full submission **(hupotage [hoop-ot-ag-ay'])** refers again to the humble state of mind of the learner. In this context, these qualities apply to the manner of learning, receiving knowledge, and understanding. Paul wants the women, as with any pupil, to have humble hearts when learning, accepting the Word taught to them in an attitude of receiving.

1 Tim. 2:12

"And I do not permit a woman to teach or to have <u>authority</u> over a man, but to be in silence". (Emphasis mine)

In this next part, most of the misunderstanding hinges on ONE Greek verb in this text – the word translated "authority."

831 authenteo { ow-then-teh'-o} which has come to mean

AV - usurp authority over 1; 1
1) one who with his own hands kills another
    or himself
2) one who acts on his own authority, autocratic

                    Can Women Teach?

3)   an absolute master
4)   to govern, exercise dominion over one

This word appears only this one time in the entire Bible. In the study of languages, translators learn the meaning of a word by studying it in several different contexts especially in comparative literature in other parts of the same book. In order to understand this word, since it only appears once in the Bible, we must go outside the Book. The meaning of this word changed over the centuries.

This is not unusual. We have seen the meaning of words change dramatically just in our lifetime. Take for instance the word "gay" — it once meant "to be happy". How about the word the young people use today to describe when they really like something - they say, "that's bad". Or how about the word "cool"? Scriptural words go through the same metamorphosis. For example, in the scripture:

Matthew 19:14

But Jesus said, Suffer little children, and forbid them
not, to come unto me: for of such is the kingdom
of heaven.

Jesus certainly didn't mean for the children to suffer, experience pain, in this text. In this text the word means to let, allow, permit. Just a few years later we would never use the word suffer when we mean let, allow, or permit.

In the classical period of Greek literature (around the 6th century BC), the word authenteo meant to initiate — be responsible for a murder or suicide. At about

200 BC the word took on new meaning. "Because suicide involves deciding for oneself, the word came to mean "self-willed" or "arbitrary:", interfering in what was not properly one's own domain, trespassing beyond the socially proper limits."[8] During the time of Christ the word oftentimes meant to be the author, or to be the originator, or to claim to be the author or the originator of something. If you write a book, you are the originator of that book and therefore have ownership of it. During the time the epistles were being penned, the word came to mean originator or creator, authentic. It wasn't until the third or fourth century that it came to mean to rule, or to have authority.

Paul used this obscure word which translators have rendered authority when he could have used a more easily understood word. He spoke of authority often but never in any other place did he use this particular word. Why? He was addressing one single situation. He was speaking specifically to the false doctrine, the heresy that the woman was the possessor of special knowledge that she received from the serpent and she was the originator of the race. She is not the "authenteo" or the originator of the race or the illuminator.

So in:

1 Timothy 2:12

And I do not permit a woman to teach or to have authority over a man, but to be in silence.

Paul was not saying that women could "never teach" or that he never permitted a woman to teach. He was saying in the verb used *"ouk epitrepo'*, "I am not permitting, for this place, time and circumstance." The verb emphasizes the temporary nature of this particular instruction. It is a verb in the present active grammatical tense which indicates a "now" thing, "at this time". Having come against the Gnostic teaching and the "false doctrine" of Eve being the originator of the race, he was instructing Timothy to not let the women teach this heresy that was proliferating in Ephesus. They were not to argue the genealogies, or bring confusion based on their misunderstandings.

The New Testament Greek could more accurately be rendered: "Let a woman quietly learn, without interruptions and questions. Presently I am not permitting (present tense for that situation) a woman to teach or proclaim herself to be the originator (authenteo) of man, but to be reverent and peaceful, coming into agreement with Scripture".

This translation fits the context, is true to the Greek, it speaks to the situation, and it lines up perfectly with all of Paul's other teachings and practices concerning women. F. F. Bruce confirms the temporary nature of the injunction not to teach in his essay, *Women in the Church: A Biblical Survey.* He summed up his dissertation by advocating that "whatever in Paul's teaching promotes true freedom is of universal and permanent validity; whatever seems to impose restrictions on true freedom has regard to local and temporary conditions."[9]

The next verse confirms this. Why would Paul even mention Adam and Eve if he were just prohibiting women from teaching? This is the scripture that completely nullifies the heresy that was being perpetrated.

1 Timothy 2:13-14

"For Adam was formed first, then Eve. And Adam was not deceived, but the woman being deceived, fell into transgression".

Paul says Adam was formed first, then Eve. That comes against all the false doctrine that was in Ephesus at that time. And he goes on to say that Eve was deceived, which comes against the doctrine that Eve was the illuminator, the teacher of new revelation. In just these two statements, Paul destroys the strongholds of Gnosticism and the Artemus cult which elevated Eve to the place held by Adam — the first human, father of the human race.

As a new Christian reading the Word and attempting to gain understanding, I viewed Paul as narrow minded and bigoted. But with revelation from the Holy Spirit, the truth of God's Word always prevails. Paul was an advocate of women teaching, preaching, prophesying, leading, being deacons, elders, and carrying out all functions that God ordains for His body. He was looking for women who would teach the truth, not false doctrine of men and demons. There are cults today that have arisen and are once again following the doctrine of Artemus such as the Lilith movement, the move to deify Mary, Wicca,[10] the manifestation of the Jezebel spirit, and others. This Word stands today as it did 2000 years ago dispelling false doctrines and revealing the truth. This Word will always be relevant to stand against false doctrine, but it should not be applied across the church for all women. Frank Viola sums up the argument over 1 Timothy 2:11-14 by saying:

> Paul's arguments, therefore, have nothing
> to do with ministry. They rather have to do
> with order in the meetings. He is arguing
> for proper order where there exists disor-
> derliness.
> Paul's message is one that promotes radi-
> cal freedom rather than suppression. And
> that freedom liberally extends to women.
> Men are in dire need of women to show
> them Christ.[11]

Just as men, filled with the Spirit of God, reveal Christ to a desperately sinful and needy world, so must Spirit-filled women. There is no longer now "male or female" for all are one in Christ. To deny a woman the right to teach would imply that she has nothing of worth to share. If a woman can be filled with the Spirit of God just as a man, then she must be allowed to bring forth the revelation she receives from the Father. Any idea that God could not or would not speak through a woman simply because she is female contradicts the whole New Testament teaching of Jesus Christ and the apostle Paul. God calls no person, male or female, on the basis of sex, but on the basis of commitment to Him.

Why has this mistranslation of one passage of the New Testament not been brought to our attention over hundreds of years of church history? What better way for Satan to attack and demean women (whom he intensely hates as the source of "the seed" that would bruise his head) than to perpetrate this great deception? A frontal attack is always too obvious. Being a liar and the father of lies, Satan chose a subtler but wholly effective means of keeping women powerless, ineffective, and under subjection. Men translated the Bible, and men interpreted Scripture based on their understanding of this male dominated structure called the Church. The mistranslation lined up with cultural prejudices of the time and no one had reason to question it. The spiritual separation that occurred in the Garden between the genders was the means for Satan to easily influence man's understanding of certain Scriptures. Many men have even questioned their own understanding, knowing in their heart that something didn't ring true. But men and women have for too long blindly accepted someone else's interpretation of Scripture. We must all take up the challenge of seeking the Holy Spirit for wisdom and discernment of truth.

Some of the father's in the faith from whom we derive a great deal of our understanding of Christian doctrine had unscriptural and ungodly things to say about women that contributed to the Church's bias. Ben Witherington III discovered this fact in his research. He relates that Tertullian (AD 160-225) had a:

> ...rather negative view of human sexuality in general, and women in particular. Besides holding Eve responsible for the original sin and identifying all women with Eve ('You, O woman, are Eve ... the gate of the devil, the traitor of the tree. You are the one who enticed the one whom the devil did not dare approach'), Tertullian adds, '...you broke...the image of God, man (homineim); because of the death you deserved the Son of God had to die.[12]

Clement of Alexandria (AD 150-215) "associates men with action, maturity, and non-castration; women with passivity, immaturity, and castration."[13] Trombley expounds this even further when he refers to the teaching of Letha Scanzoni and Nancy Hardesty in the book *All We're Meant To Be*. He says that according to their research based on hormonal evidence, the perception in our society is that:

> ...the mentally healthy male is aggressive, independent, unemotional, logical, direct, adventurous, self-confident and ambitious while the mentally healthy female is passive, emotional, dependent, less competitive, nonobjective, submissive, vain, easily influenced, religious and insecure. The male traits are called adult or mature while the female traits are called childish or neurotic.[14]

Below are further examples of the erroneous teachings perpetrated throughout the church. We are grateful to Charles Trombley for his many years of thorough research that brought these errors to light.

- Origen: All women were the opposite of spirit; therefore, they were earthly, fleshly and evil.

- Tertullian: Saw woman as a personification of fundamentally evil sex and men as the innocent victims of feminine wiles.

- Augustine: Decided women weren't created in God's image, only men were.

- John Calvin: Taught that women were created inferior and must be ruled by men. Therefore, he reasoned, men were created to control and rule women. He also commented on the scripture in 1 Tim. 2:12 by saying, women are by nature born to obey men. What he implied was, "Men are by nature born to govern and control women."

o Martin Luther expressed similar attitudes.

o Josephus wrote, "the woman, says the law, is in all things inferior to the man. Let her accordingly be submissive". He was referring to the oral law, not the Torah or the written law of God, which is the only authority.[15]

We are not looking for women's equality, women's rights, or to fill a quota of women in leadership. What we are looking for is Jesus incarnate in people — male or female. We are looking for His nature, His character, those who share His suffering, His humility, and His obedience. Paul says when you employ widows look for those who have washed the feet of the saints for in them you will see Jesus.

Jesus is looking for those who have submitted themselves to the discipline of God. He is looking for His holiness, His wisdom, His authority, His sacrificial love, and His anointing that breaks the yoke. This is about Jesus; it is about Jesus incarnate in men and women; it is about Jesus shining forth His light in and through all of us.

The time has come to break the yoke of fear, of bondage, of enmity between men and women, of oppression, of bitterness, of prejudice and distorted teaching. In order to break a yoke, however, we must first admit that one binds us. The next chapter deals with this issue from a male perspective.

Chapter Five Notes

[1] Boyd, Gregory. *Christianity & Culture: Women In Ministry #1*: (Christus Victor Ministries). p 1 of 3. Online. Internet 13 March 2002

[2] Tetlow, Elizabeth M. *Women and Ministry in the New Testament.* (New York, NY: Paulist Press, 1980). p 140.

[3] Boyd, Gregory. *Christianity & Culture: Women In Ministry #2*: (Christus Victor Ministries). p 1 of 3. Online. Internet 13 March 2002.

[4] IBID. p 2 of 3

[5] Jacobs, Cindy. *Women of Destiny.* (Ventura, Calif.: Regal Books, 1998) p. 184.

[6] Viola, Frank. *Now Concerning A Woman's Role In The Church. An Open Letter.* p 5, Online. Internet 6 March 2002.

[7] Trombley, Charles. *Who Said Women Can't Teach?* (South Plainfield, NJ: Bridge Publishing, Inc., 1985). p 170.

[8] IBID. p 174.

[9] Bruce, F.F. *A Mind for What Matters Collected Essays* (Grand Rapids, MI; Wm. B. Eerdmans Publishing Co, 1990), p 263.

[10] Wicca is a Neo-paganism organization practicing "white" witchcraft, using elements of Freemasonry, Celtic pagan practices, and other sources of soulish power. A couple of years ago, an article appeared in <u>Charisma</u> magazine wherein a reporter had gone undercover in Wiccan covens. It was sadly discovered that a great majority of Wiccan participants were "church" rejects who had left their Christian heritage because of prejudice and judgment in the churches.

[11] Viola. p 18.

[12] Witherington, Ben III. *Women in the Earliest Churches.* (New York, NY: Cambridge University Press. 1988). pp 185-186.

[13] IBID. p187.

[14] Trombley. P 82.

[15] IBID. pp 202-206.

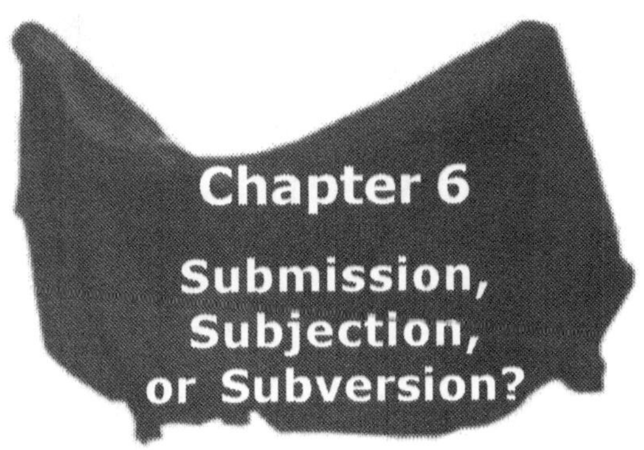

By William Cassada

In preparation for writing this chapter, I recently came across a most revealing comment regarding women in ministry. The comment was made in response to an article that appeared in Christianity Today (4/8/96) quoting a popular contemporary speaker and author who is also the wife of a pastor of a rather large church.   In the article, she was quoted as saying, "...and for eight years I preached and taught and saw people come to Christ on the streets..." The author of this website had the following comment regarding her account:

> ...the fact that people were saved in her preaching does not mean that God gives His stamp of approval to it. The end does not justify the means.... (a Scriptural reference, Phil. 1:15-18 was given to justify this observation)[1]

The comment is revealing because it represents a very common and widely held bias about women in ministry – basically it's a sort of "who do they think they are" kind of mentality. This comment also reflects the theological brain fog that, unfortunately, envelops a large segment of the church. (I say "brain fog" because it implies a deception, which it is. The deceiver has blinded our eyes to the truth. A few men may have used the accepted translation of certain scriptures for their own egotistical agendas; but most men who adhere to this philosophy that truly love God are not power hungry, just deceived.) It is interesting to note that in somewhat of a "2 Corinthians 4:4 kind of blindness," the very words that the Apostle Paul wrote, used by the above quoted writer to justify his observation, actually encourage preaching of the gospel by anyone, anywhere! In verse 18 Paul writes, *"I've decided that I really don't care about their motives, whether mixed, bad, or indifferent. Every time one of them opens his mouth, Christ is proclaimed, so I just cheer them on!"*[2]

Clark Pinnock, writing in *The Openness Of God*, spoke about the result of the coupling of biblical ideas about God with notions of the divine nature drawn from the Greek, and accurately observed that it resulted in many significant insights and helped to evangelize the pagan culture during the early church period. But he also observes:

> Along with the good, however, came a certain theological virus that infected the Christian doctrine of God, making it ill and creating all sorts of problems...The virus so permeates Christian theology that some have

come to take the illness for granted, attrib-
uting it to divine mystery, while others re-
main unaware of the infection altogether.[3]

Because of the broad influence of Greek philosophy (pagan, cerebral, analytical thinking) on many of the
church's founding fathers and the formulation of early
church doctrine which serves as much of our Christian
Biblical foundations, it would appear that the "theological
virus" that Pinnock speaks of is still with us in some form
or another.

With no intent to personally attack this commenter,
the character of his remarks do represent the brand of
arrogant, egocentristic, attitudes which are present in
much of the global church. We sometimes forget when
people get saved just exactly who it is that is doing the
saving. It would be a theological error of gigantic proportions if we assumed that anyone came into the Kingdom of God because of our eloquence, talent, ability, or
any other attribute. If we sincerely believe that it is some
great talent that we personally possess that is winning
people to Christ, we deceive ourselves in the utmost
manner. Clearly it is the Holy Spirit, moving upon people's
hearts, that bring them to Jesus Christ, and we must
never forget that.

Ted Wise, writing about the late Lonnie Frisbee,
his friend and also a very controversial minister, gives us
more to ponder along these lines.

On the first day of the outreach we had
managed to nearly fill the theater with nonbelievers. I brought my co-workers from
PBC and my teenaged daughter Erin to the

meeting. Erin had known and loved Lonnie for almost ten years. He used to read bedtime stories to her during the House of Acts days. She also had a growing appreciation of Dr. Ray Stedman's exposition of the Scriptures and had not heard Lonnie preach for some time. Lonnie gave a very simple talk from the Gospel of John and ended the meeting with an alter (sic) call. My daughter, who had been drawing in her sketch pad suddenly looked up in alarm, it seemed to her that her friend Lonnie was going to embarrass himself big time. She said, "Dad, doesn't he know no one's going to get up and go forward?" Much to her and my fellow expositors' surprise, a large teary eyed crowd went to the front of the theater to pray for forgiveness and to receive the Lord Jesus into their hearts.

Later, at our house my daughter asked Lonnie how could he do something so daring as inviting people to stand up and go forward in front of all their friends. Wasn't he scared nothing could happen? I overheard Lonnie's truthful answer, "It's a gift from God Erin, I could say Mary had a little lamb, anybody want to accept Christ as their savior and they would all get up and come forward." Lonnie went on to explain how the Holy Spirit had been preparing and drawing people to the theater and [to] receive Christ for days maybe even years before the meeting took place.[4]

Historically and theologically, Lonnie Frisbee was an extremely controversial character. He was very nontraditional, sometimes described as "weird," and he often made people nervous during his preaching. People would often say to him, "Lonnie, what you're preaching is not in the Bible," to which he would reply, "so what?" As strange as Lonnie was, he obviously recognized "from whence his strength cometh." He knew it was the anointing of the Holy Spirit and not himself, and much to the chagrin of many of those who witnessed his preaching, he was very much at ease in this role. For a man who professed to have met Jesus personally while wandering naked in the desert, he probably didn't allow traditionalism to get in his way.

In another account written about Lonnie, David DiSabatino makes this observation in an article posted on Richard Riss' Awakening Email List a few years ago:

> One of the things that David DiSabatino observes in his paper is that some people felt that there was very little relationship between any real fullness of content in Lonnie Frisbee's messages and the release of the power of God at the times that he ministered. He quoted Chuck Smith's comments one night when Lonnie was speaking at Calvary Chapel, to the effect that "there was no content whatsoever to the message he was bringing...But just watch! It will be the biggest night we have in terms of what God does."[5]

Eureka! Isn't that what we all strive for in ministry, to see God move? If so, then why are we so afraid of the type of "package" that brings us into God's presence? Is the North American church doing such a good job that we all think we have arrived at some sort of state of perfection where we can be so selective about who brings the anointing into our midst?

The State Of The American Church

The American Church has systematically excluded women from occupying any real leadership roles mainly through its biased interpretations and misunderstanding of Paul's New Testament writings concerning women. Perhaps it's time we issued the church a report card to see how well this subjection and subversion of God's intentions for women has served us. Consider these sobering comments from some contemporary authors about the condition of the church:

Frank Viola, *ReThinking The Wineskin:*

...the institutional church is essentially a nursery for overgrown spiritual babes. Because it has habituated God's people into being passive receivers, it has stunted their spiritual development and kept them in spiritual infancy...while the church has claimed the ground of a believing priesthood, it has failed to occupy that ground.

Consequently, in the typical Protestant church, the doctrine of the priesthood of all believers is no more than a sterile truth...a doctrine in modern evangelicalism that continues to beg for practical application and implementation in the life of the Lord's people...[6]

Howard Eberle, *The Complete Wineskin:*

Whether we like it or not, our religious traditions are well-established...
...the Apostolic anointing has been replaced

by superintendents, district representatives, overseers, bishops, and others with various titles...the prophetic voice has been replaced by doctrinal statements and other accepted forms of practice.[7]

Tommy Tenney, *The God-Catchers*:

We spend entire lifetimes sitting in pews but leave the four walls of our churches and make no impact on our world whatsoever...[8]

For too long the church has trumpeted to the nations, "He's here! He's here!" When the reality has been that there's not been enough of His Presence in our churches to make them discernibly different from the world.[9]

Jonas Clark, *Governing Churches And Antioch Apostles*:

We've had two thousand years to reach this world for Jesus...So what's the problem? Could it be that we have created a religious system that in effect has caused us to be ineffective?[10]

In reality we have created a structure of church services that is designed to gather, entertain, and baby-sit immature believers.[11]

The religious church is a man-motivated, dead, works-oriented, soulish, carnal church with only a form of godliness; but without Holy Ghost leadership, revelation, inspiration, and power.[12]

Roger Helland, pastor of Kelowna BC Vineyard, writing in *The Revived Church:*

> While the majority of Canadians, Americans and the British say they believe in God, most want nothing to do with the Church or organized religion...People want God but don't want church...The church (especially in the Western world) is largely powerless.[13]

Dr. Michael L. Brown, writing for Randy Clark in his book, *Power, Holiness & Evangelism* poses the question, "why do so many Christian converts bear so few marks of conversion; and why do so many saints seem so unsaintly?" - or to put it another way, "why do so many of our churches seem to be filled with the semi-saved" Dr. Brown quotes James Edwin Orr who concludes:

> It is primarily the result of spiritual birth defects. In other words, these woefully shallow, hardly committed, almost always lukewarm believers — "saved" though they may be — are the product of a defective gospel message. And so, because our gospel message has been defective, our disciples are now defective and the American "born-again" church is defective as well. This is a vicious cycle of "genetically" flawed reproduction with far reaching consequences.[14]

Graham Cooke writes in his book, *A Divine Confrontation:*

> We have allowed a superficial mass production of people to come into the church where we are not adequately equipped to deal with

the problems that keep arising. We produce a mutant breed of genetically engineered believers with a weird theology that is counterproductive to the work and practice of the Holy Spirit.[15]

We still have a most unbiblical void between the clergy and laity. Many believers are still treated as pew fodder every week, as they are fed a diet of one-man ministry, irrelevant sermons, and little or no supernatural expression, experience, or expectation.[16]

We've gone about as far as we can go in our present level of understanding about the work of the church, strategies for reaching the harvest, and the deployment of gifts and personnel. We have hit the ceiling of revelatory insight under our present church methods and cannot go further without a most radical change of heart.[17]

Dr. Bill Bright comments (as qtd. in Helland, p 32):

...having fallen into the cult of the comfortable, the church, for the most part, is no longer a power to be reckoned with.[18]

Jim Henderson, host of the recently formed "Off The Map" (OTM) Movement[19], has this to say:

...with more Americans dismissing the relevance of traditional Christianity to their lives...it is time for a major change in the way believers try to share their faith...too few Christians are actively involved in evangelism because of what the church has made it...

> ...We turn people outside the church into enemies with whom we are engaged in warfare, not lost sheep for whom the Shepherd cares and to whom we have been sent...
>
> ...[Church is] not something they notice...if the mall and the church disappeared tomorrow, which would people miss most? ...the answer speaks to the irrelevancy of our institutions in our culture...[20]

Over the past two thousand years, Christians have managed to reshape and remodel the church into a place of barrenness, travesty, and cultural irrelevance.

Instead of being focused on the fulfillment of God's commission to proclaim the Kingdom of God, many of us have been more concerned about reinforcing the dogmas and practices of our ecclesiastical structures, the entrenchment of denominational identities, and ensuring the persecution and ridicule of those who may have opposing beliefs, especially concerning the submission, subjection, and subversion of the role of women in ministry.

The church today has had such little effect on society that our moral foundations have crumbled to the point that abortion is rampant, homosexuality is becoming increasingly acceptable as an alternative lifestyle, and unconscionable acts of sexual immorality have occurred in the highest office in our land.

In our own ministry experiences, we've found that many churches look more like hospitals and nurseries where the lame, the sick, and the spiritually crippled come week after week to nurse their wounds and infirmities, and to have their diapers changed. In truth, these "hospital" churches have become hospices where tired, wounded, and burned out pastors tend to the needs of their dying flocks. One pastor we know jokingly remarked one Sunday morning that he was guilty of "necromancy," i.e., "having relations with the dead (His congregation)."

These candid and revealing assessments of the condition of the church by well-known and respected authors should themselves be enough of a wake-up call. However, there are even far more serious problems plaguing the church, such as the recent multi-million dollar lawsuit settlements by the Catholic church, paid on behalf of multitudes of previously hidden but now discovered child-molesting priests, not to mention the almost daily news articles of pastors and church leaders across the country who are involved in some kind of sexual immorality.[21]

Russell Shaw observes: "After twenty-five years of institutional decline, the Catholic Church in the United States may now be entering an era of institutional collapse. Nearly every indicator of anything that can be measured and quantified suggests as much."[22]

Ralph Martin writing in, *The Catholic Church At The End Of An Age*, chronicled a church system crumbling before our very eyes, but nothing in its previous history has brought so much decimation into the church as the recent scandalous revelations concerning sexual molestation of children by its clergy. The entire issue of celibacy among the priesthood, an unscriptural doctrine of the Catholic Church, is now being brought into question by its leadership.

Not confined solely to the Catholic Church, Scripture has been all but forgotten in some other major mainline denominations as homosexual priests are   being ordained, and relationships between practicing homosexuals are being blessed by liberal church officials.

And finally, a theologian from a mainstream Protestant seminary offers the coup-de-grace:

> ...Disregard of God's Laws has resulted in a drug war that we are not winning, in burgeoning crime that has made neighborhoods uninhabitable, in teenage pregnancies and 'children having children', in rampant abortions, swelling welfare rolls, sexually transmitted diseases, self-indulgent neglect of community good, and countless ruined lives. We chose our own way and...brought ourselves to the way of death.[23]

If we truly will take a step back and look at our current system of what we call "church" and really examine and scrutinize it to see how it conforms to God's prototype, we may be in for a few surprises. Many of the current practices and activities that take up most of our time and energy in churches have no Biblical foundation.

It certainly doesn't take a rocket scientist to figure out that something is dreadfully wrong with our system of church. Filled with meaningless programs, seething with back-room immorality, faithfully attended by spiritually immature believers, many of them physically infirm or emotionally imprisoned, much of the church has become the laughing stock of our society. One of the common definitions of insanity is to continue doing the same thing over and over again, but hoping for different results. It is high time that we examined how we do church and make a few course adjustments.

You Don't Send Me Flowers

Because of the male-dominated hierarchy in our North American church system, the "intellectual" rather than "spiritual" application of scripture that sometimes forms our theological doctrines and practices has been used to dominate, manipulate, control, and suppress women for hundreds of years. Here's a quick and simple test to determine if your study and understanding of Scripture is on the money – does your understanding and interpretation of the Bible serve to liberate? – or does it place people in bondage? Unfortunately, much of our contemporary and historical understanding, interpretation, and application of the Bible towards women's issues, has only served to imprison instead of liberate. The acceptance of this mere fact alone is enough to prompt us to thoroughly re-examine our interpretation of Scripture. Was God just making a joke when He said in 1 John 2:27 "you need not that any man teach you?" I think not. And women have paid the price dearly because we have looked to intellect for the answers and not to the Holy Spirit.

One of the main reasons for the church-wide suppression of women is that men tend to think hierarchically. Men, as a result of the fallen nature, like being in charge, they like being "over" others, and easily fall into the exegetical trap that only men can be in positions of authority and leadership within the church. My personal experience is that the default position of much of the church is to accept what it has been given in its original form, without checking out or verifying what has been handed down to them from the pulpit. In my own case, it was only as the Holy Spirit began to reveal these things to me that I could take a step back and begin to re-examine every aspect of the religious system that I grew up with.

The Church:
Ecclesiastical Tower of Discrimination
or Equal Opportunity Employer?

Examine if you will, Ephesians 4:8-13. This passage speaks of five different types of ministry. As you're reading this, you're probably already thinking of the term "five-fold" ministry. But that term does not appear anywhere in those Scripture passages, which is one of the problems we deal with. Writer Brad Pliam comments on what has become a blueprint in the church for implementing God's system of church authority –

> ...till we ALL come to the measure of the stature of the fullness of Christ... Yet, the context really seems to speak of something that will be happening to ALL of us "men" [and women]. Nothing wrong with the blue-print concept, but the perversion of it is something that has sadly led to false hierarchical systems, where "pastors" as we know them are made to be subjugated to the even higher-up Apostle. Well, this verse actually SHOULD be our blueprint for church government. The key is that there is NO entrenched hierarchy...but they are all to be submitted to in the same way we submit to ANYONE speaking or moving under the rule of the HOLY SPIRIT. [Emphasis added][24]

Almost everyone thinks of the "five-fold" ministry as a hierarchical structure with Apostles at the top and teachers at the bottom. There have been innumerable doctrines, philosophies, and ministries spawned from this hierarchical interpretation, which does nothing to further unity and the cause of Christ, but serves only to subjugate and dominate.

Actually when the Bible speaks of Apostles in the book of Ephesians (2:20), it says, "Apostles and Prophets are *foundations* and that Jesus Christ is the chief *cornerstone*". The last time I saw a building being erected, I distinctly remember that the foundation was poured at the very bottom of the structure. When the building is completed, most of the foundation remains underground and not visible to the naked eye. Instead of being established in a super-minister overseer kind of role that many of today's apostolic ministries have become, the true Biblical role of an apostle is not to be in the forefront, but to be nearly invisible, to work behind the scenes, to father, not control. The cornerstone of most buildings is also located near the bottom, not on the rooftop! Jesus continual example was of servanthood in leadership. Lower is better. God does the exalting.

In the Biblical account of Jesus' encounter with the Roman Centurion, (Mt 8:9; Lk 7:8) the underlying significance lies in the fact that the centurion recognized that Jesus' power to do the things He was doing was because He was *under authority* — not exercising power over others, nor lording it over them, so to speak, but *under authority*. Jesus was living out the very principles of the Word of God, *"The more lowly your service to others, the greater you are. To be the greatest, be a servant."*[25]

We have not only imposed on the church a hierarchical understanding of what the five-fold ministry is all about, but have at the same time, elevated these male-dominated positions to the rooftop, while women's roles have been relegated to the underground vaults. We tell women its okay to teach children's church, but when it comes to overseeing the spiritual lives of adults, that task is left primarily to the men.

Using this same philosophy, we have (at least until recently with the resurgence of the prophetic and apostolic) also pushed out and virtually eliminated any influence of the apostolic and prophetic offices in most of our churches, so that pastors (most of whom are male) now almost exclusively maintain the spiritual lives of their church members, and their "office" has been elevated to a place the Bible never intended, and one that no man could possibly fill.[26] Although many in the body are once again acknowledging and seeking the contributions of apostles and prophets, the larger percentage of the church still avoids their ministry.

The Scripture passage referred to above, Ephesians 2:20, actually speaks to the work of Jesus, "...who being found in fashion as a man, he humbled himself..." (Phil. 2:8) Carnal man, on the other hand, desires power and control, and wants to have authority over others. In bringing into the church over the last several thousand years this kind of hierarchical chain-of-command type of thinking, it has been rather simple to deny the gifting and anointing of those who don't fit into this self-made system. Consequently women have not only been the unwilling victims of such a system, but have fallen easy prey to it. God has a structure, accountability, leadership; but His way is based on humility, servanthood, and unfailing love.

The hierarchical power-based system we've built into our church governments has stifled the effectiveness of the offices that God Himself set in the church and the repression of women has been one of it's lethal byproducts.

Hupotasso

Much of the misunderstanding, misinterpretation, and misapplication of God's intent regarding the issue of subjection has been drawn from a skewed perspective that comes from applying a cerebral viewpoint instead of a spiritual one to the definition of subjection.

The Greek word that is most often translated "submit" in the New Testament is the word **hupotasso**. A much better translation of this word is "subjection." Subjection, as it is used in the New Testament, is a voluntary attitude of giving in, cooperating with, and yielding to the admonition of another. What is important to recognize here is that God's perspective of "subjection" is from the bottom up, whereas man's perspective always seems to be from the top down. Carnal man wants to dominate and control, and will not miss an opportunity to position himself as "king of the hill" when it comes to subjection and submission. God's perspective is more like being at the bottom looking up, and having a child-like way of thinking, open to the insight and introspection of others, and with an attitude of mutual subjection towards them as they reflect the mind of Christ.

Author Frank Viola puts it this way:

> Because the church is an extended household, a circular model of power and authority is to be followed rather than a vertical one. The NT approach to church leadership emphasizes power *for* and power *among* rather than power *over;* the empowerment of all rather than the empowerment of a few...servitude rather than dominance.[27]

Christianity's traditional approach to the meaning and application of these issues has produced ecclesiastical, institutional, denominational, and theological viewpoints of what subjection is all about and generally has placed men at the top as superior and women at the bottom as inferior. But in God's society, divine authority is expressed through mutual subjection and shared power, through teamwork, and *one-anothering,* not through some hierarchical structure. His design for the church has always been that it be a participatory society wherein Divine Authority flows to and through *anyone who possesses the Spirit, regardless of gender.*

For many years, people have felt "uncomfortable" with the gender-biased church-wide treatment of Biblical subjects such as submission and authority. Church leaders' counsel for wives to submit themselves to their husbands in every conceivable kind of ungodly behavior represents an irresponsible oversight of the flock and one which has destroyed many lives and families. At other times, we have sat silently by, knowing that what was being taught about the controversial "women" passages represented contradiction, conflict, and misunderstanding. But the greater church has allowed it to go on. I agree with Barbara's assessment that if it is carnal man's interpretation of these Scriptures which promulgate confusion through theological error, and allow the continuation of a male-dominated system of leadership within the church, then why would any man want to change them? Even if he wanted to, the deception perpetrated by Satan has blinded so much of the church. The doctrine of women being second-class citizens has served the purposes of a dominating male headship for many centuries. Of course, a truly Spirit led person who humbles themselves, seeking after truth will find it. Many have. And for those that have, the revelation is that Christ places the leadership in the church. When man chooses leaders rather than God, his choices will generally be drawn from the fallen nature and the criteria used will ultimately be carnal.

What's The Answer?

For the first fifteen years of our marriage, quite frankly, Barbara and I struggled. It was the second marriage for both of us, and we were both independent, dominating, and opinionated. I'm not really sure how we survived, but somehow we did, and it was only when God began to turn our relationship around that things began to get better. I have to make a long story really short here, but I think the major turning point was one day when I was driving home and talking to the Lord about Barbara. At this time, we both had been experiencing a spiritual awakening in our personal lives as well as in our relationship. God was doing something in our hearts.

As I walked in to the house through the garage, I was saying to God, "Lord, I really do love Barbara – I just don't know how to express it." Up until this time, I had pretty well done everything in our relationship my way, but now it seemed that God was really working me over. In that crystal clear unmistakable speaking of Spirit-to-spirit, I heard the Lord say to me, "OK, are you finally ready to let ME teach you how to love your wife? – if you are, then I will teach you to love your wife as Christ loved the church and gave Himself for it."

I was blown away. I knew this was God, but it all sounded a little radical. As I walked into the kitchen of our New Jersey home, the Lord continued speaking to me. "You've been arrogant concerning her wishes in this house," He said. "You've not allowed her to exercise the femininity and womanness that I created in her within the home." I stopped in my tracks, speechless. "Let her put the salt and pepper shakers where she wants them, and let her decide where things are best put in the kitchen." I was stunned. Was this the way it was going to be, I thought? But it was, and it was from that moment the changes began. (Despise not small beginnings!) In thinking back to this time, I suppose I had to finally get to that place of desperation and frustration at my own unsuccessful attempts to repair our marriage. But God began with the simplest things, and began to show me that I had to allow Barbara to be the person that God created her to be, not the one that I wanted her to be. I had been making the same mistake the church has made for hundreds of years.

It was almost comical in the days that followed. Barbara will tell you that she began to notice the changes almost immediately, but she was suspicious. She wondered how I could change so dramatically, and because of our track record, she was reluctant to accept the "new me." But over time the changes stuck and our relationship has improved dramatically since then.

We've learned from our ministry experiences that whenever we go to a new place to hold meetings, our first clue to knowing what condition the church is in, is to observe the relationship of the pastor and their spouse. How the man treats the woman in their relationship speaks volumes about his effectiveness in shepherding God's people. Is the wife merely a figurehead, making sure that dinner is served on time, and that all the necessary menial tasks in the church and home are accomplished? Or is she a viable and equal leadership partner, providing insight into daily decision-making and influencing the growth of the flock through her God-given abilities and talents?

If we are going to overcome the mistakes of the past, we must learn to work together as men and women, each of us of drawing on the gifts and anointings that God has placed on and within us, without fear of the other's successes. We must relinquish the egocentric, arrogant, and machoistic perspective that as men, we have all the answers, we can handle anything, and we don't need anyone's help. This kind of thinking is what has brought us to the place we are now. We have to change our "stinking thinking" and recognize that we are only going to be able to accomplish God's purposes TOGETHER! We must learn to allow our gifts and talents to compliment each other instead of competitively trying to maintain the hierarchical edge. We must learn to allow the abilities of others to find their own levels, and when appropriate, to rise to the surface of their own accord. How dare we in our carnal human self-centered efforts attempt to suppress the very anointing of God that rests on another person? And why do we care if the person is Jew, Greek, Black, White, Purple, Man, Woman, or donkey? The Bible offers ample evidence that God can accomplish His purposes in any way He chooses.[28]

Our historical and ecclesiastical view of what forms church leadership and authority should take has served to elevate carnal man and has stifled and suppressed gifted women. We must change our perspective, otherwise how can we expect God to bless our activities? We must open our spiritual eyes and "see what the Father is doing." If what we see the Father doing is anointing women for ministry, then we need to acknowledge that God has a much better view of all this than we have.

In our own marriage relationship, once we allowed the Holy Spirit to rule and reign over our lives and partnership, we recognized that we are a team. There is not a lesson plan, sermon, teaching, or book that has been written by either of us that has not been reviewed by the other. We value each other's opinions and perspectives. We recognize that we both have different abilities, and we must bring all of them to bear in order to be the effective team that God has called us to be. Barbara has the academic brain, the understanding of physics, the scientific mind, the feminine intuition, the prophetic insight, and other traits that God has blessed her with. She hears God on a different level and in a different way than I do. I, on the other hand, am a much more pragmatic, down-to-earth kind of person; but I recognize that I need her input, her perspective, and her insight. I am not threatened by her success or by the gifts that God has given her. She is a powerful preacher, obviously anointed by God, and she has preached me to tears on more than one occasion. When she preaches, she is not my wife or the Barbara that I know in that context, but she is simply someone on whom the power and anointing of God rests. Why can't we all learn to recognize and acknowledge that if God has placed His anointing and His blessing on a woman, then maybe – just maybe – we need to go back to Scripture and re-examine our understanding and interpretation of the "women" verses; the ones which carnal men have used for so long to hold women in prison instead of liberating them and allowing them to enjoy the freedom of operating in the gifts and callings that God gave them?

We have for the most part, due to the deception perpetrated by our enemy, made church exactly what our cerebral and self-centered ways of thinking have wanted it to be, i.e., dismissing the apostolic and the prophetic as irrelevant, and suppressing the giftings of the female gender. But God is changing the face of the church. Its time we got on board with what He is doing, not what our world-influenced, politically and culturally correct thoughts are telling us.

If someone as different and as controversial as a Lonnie Frisbee could draw thousands of young people to the Lord, with, as many of his critics have said, "no real fullness of content in his messages," how much more credibility should we place on women who preach powerfully, who move in the anointing and power of God, and who are often cloaked with the kabod (Heb. kābôd, *with the root idea of 'heaviness' and so of 'weight')* of God?

A Nigerian bishop, Gabriel Ganaka, puts it this way:

> We need the power of the Holy Spirit and the focus on the person of Jesus that Peter had in the early days of the church, as described in the Acts of the Apostles; on one day Peter preached one sermon and three thousand people converted; **we preach three thousand sermons and no one converts.**[29]

Pastors, has your preaching been a little dry lately? Has it been months, maybe even years since someone got saved during one of your messages? Has the fire seemed to have gone out of your pulpit presence? Is there no expectation or manifestation of God's Presence in your church services? Is attendance down? Has giving dropped off? Has it been such a long time since you've seen anyone healed of anything in your church?

If your answer to any of these questions is "yes," then I recommend allowing your wife to preach next Sunday. You may discover, as David DiSabatino observed, "there was no content whatsoever to the message...But just watch! It will be the biggest night we have in terms of what God does."[30]

I am certainly not foolish enough to suggest that recognizing the role of women in ministry will automatically cure the church's ills. What I am saying, however, is that we have underestimated the consequences of their historical, theological, and gender-based exclusion from equal partnership in leadership roles within the global church.

Like a reluctant youngster, knowing he is sick, but

putting off the spoonful of castor oil as long as possible, so too is today's church. There are many voices saying "it's broken," but not many who are willing to apply the necessary remedies. It means we'll have to recognize women as equals (just like God does!) and allow the anointing of God that is on their lives to manifest itself as God sees fit. I can say it no better than the following prayer by Jim Goll. Let us all earnestly repent from the erroneous submission, subjection, and subversion of women in the body of Christ.

Jim Goll's Prayer

Women of the Church, you have been shackled long enough! As a man in the Church I want to confess to you that we, the men of the Body of Christ, have feared you and have clung tightly to our rights, our positions, and our functions out of the fear that we would lose them to you. In our own insecurity and sin we have been unwilling to fully recognize your gifts, calling, and anointing in the Spirit or to accept you as full equals in the life and ministry of the Church. This might sound a bit brash, but in my opinion it's time for the "good ole boys' club" to come to an end!

Therefore, I ask you, the women, to forgive us for holding you back, for not being cheerleaders for you, for not helping to equip you, and for not releasing you to fulfill God's calling on your lives. Forgive us for paying only lip service to your value, your gifts, your call, and your anointing. Forgive us for treating you like second-class citizens of the Kingdom and for not recognizing your equal status with us.

> *Father, forgive us! We have sinned and acted wickedly! We have wrongfully bound our sisters, your daughters, and held them back from full participation in the life of the Church of which they and we are equally a part. Forgive us, Lord, and release the light of revelation and change to come in Your Body. O Lord, release your daughters.*[31]

My final thoughts as I end this chapter are directed to the women who read this, not the men. Yes it's true that male-dominated thinking is responsible for much of the repression of women in our church system. But simply discovering this truth and acknowledging its devastating effects on our society is not enough. The responsibility is on you women to look to God's Word to determine your destiny, and not what a man tells you. You must not allow the biased roles, which have been handed down to you over the generations, to determine your destiny. No, you must look to God and to what He says about your role, and what He is saying is that your role is one of equal partnership. This is not a mandate for a feminist agenda, but a call for you to rise to the occasion of God's calling on your life. It's time, women, to "remove your veils!"

Chapter Six Notes

[1]Phil's Family Stuff, Epistle#30, August 1996, Internet [http://www.geocities.com/Heartland/3791/epist30.html]

[2] Philippians 1:18, The Message, © 1993, 1994, 1995 by Eugene H. Peterson, NavPress, Colorado Springs

[3] Pinnock, Clark. The Openness of God. (Downers Grove, IL: Intervarsity Press, 1994). Preface, pp. 8-9

[4] Wise, Ted, quoted on Richard M. Riss' Awakening List, February 7, 1998, Internet, Email rriss@drew.edu

[5] From David Di Sabatino's 32-page academic paper on Lonnie Frisbee, quoted on Richard M. Riss' Awakening List, December 30, 1997, Internet, Email rriss@drew.edu

[6] Viola, Frank. ReThinking The Wineskin. (Brandon, FL: Present Testimony Ministry, 1998). p. 29

[7] Eberle, Howard. The Complete Wineskin. (Yakima, WA: Winepress Publishing, 1993). pp. 85, 127

[8] Tenny, Tommy. The God-Catchers. (Nashville, TN: Thomas Nelson Publishers, 2000). p. 63

[9] Ibid, p. 109

[10] Clark, Jonas. Governing Churches & Antioch Apostles. (Hallandale, FL: Spirit of Life Publishing, 2000). p 29

[11] Ibid, p 28

[12] Ibid, p 41

[13] Helland, Roger. The Revived Church. (Kent, UK: Sovereign World, 1998).
 p 32

[14] Clark, Randy. Power, Holiness, & Evangelism. (Shippensburg, PA: Destiny Image Publishers, Inc., 1999). p 41.

[15] Cooke, Graham. A Divine Confrontation. (Shippensburg, PA: Destiny Image Publishers, Inc., 1999). p 17

[16] Ibid, p 42

[17] Ibid, p 38

[18] Bright, Dr. Bill. The Coming Revival. (NewLife Publications; 1995). p.34 quoted by Roger Helland, The Revived Church, Kent, UK, Sovereign World, 1998, p.32

[19] Henderson, Jim. quoted by Andy Butcher, Churches Need To Redefine Evangelism," Charisma News Service Update for Thursday, March 14, 2002, Charisma News Service, Vol. 4 No. 10 [http://www.charismamag.com]
"The Off the Map (OTM) movement tries to turn the accepted idea of evangelism on its head by inverting the traditional church meeting. At OTM events, the pastors and lay members sit quietly in the audience while nonbelievers take the microphone to explain their lack of faith."

[20]Ibid.

[21] Celebrated Florida Revival Church Rocked By Pastor Sex Scandal, Charisma Online News Service, June 14, 2000 edition; News

Brief: Roberts Liardon Leaves Ministry Over 'Moral Failure' CHA-RISMA NEWS SERVICE Fri, Dec 21, 2001 Vol. 3 No. 190; these are only two of the many news articles from the past several years

[22] Shaw, Russell. "Conference in Defense of Western Civilization: Response to Rev. Richard John Neuhaus", October 6, 1992 (unpublished) quoted by Ralph Martin, The Catholic Church At The End Of An Age. (San Francisco: Ignatius Press, 1998). p 37

[23] Achtamaier, Elizabeth. cited in Fellowship of Catholic Scholars Newsletter, June 1992, p. 30; quoted by Ralph Martin, The Catholic Church At The End Of An Age, (Ignatius Press: San Francisco, ,1998) p. 24.

[24] Pliam, Brad. A Legacy Of No Accountability, 2001, Internet

[25] Matthew 23:11, AMPLIFIED NEW TESTAMENT®, Copyright 1958, 1987 by The Lockman. Foundation. Used by permission

[26] The word "pastor" is used as a noun only once in the entire New Testament, (Eph. 4:11) as part of a team, and what the office has become has no foundation in Scripture, and there is no framework of reference to "pastors" within the foundations of the early church. The pastoral office in today's church has been one of the primary factors in producing a dependent culture of spiritually immature people, who rely on the paid "holy man" to be holy for them. As a result, spiritual gifts are showcased from the platform, but rarely cultivated among the church at large. Howard Eberle says, "The accepted pattern of organization for the local church is to have a pastor at the head, with the congregation involved under him in varying degrees. However, this pattern is foreign to the New Testament. Nowhere in the Bible can we find a "pastor" leading a congregation." The Complete Wineskin, Yakima, WA Winepress Publishing, 1993, p. 43

[27] Viola, Frank. Who Is Your Covering. (Brandon, FL; Present Testimony Ministry; 1999). p 65

[28] 2 Peter 2:16, The Living Bible, "...but Balaam was stopped from his mad course when his donkey spoke to him with a human voice, scolding and rebuking him..."

[29] Ganaka, Gabriel. quoted by Ralph Martin, The Catholic Church At The End Of An Age. (San Francisco; Ignatius Press; 1998). p 65

[30] Di Sabatino.

[31] Goll, Jim. Father Forgive Us. (Shippensburg, PA; Destiny Image Publishers; 1999). p 111

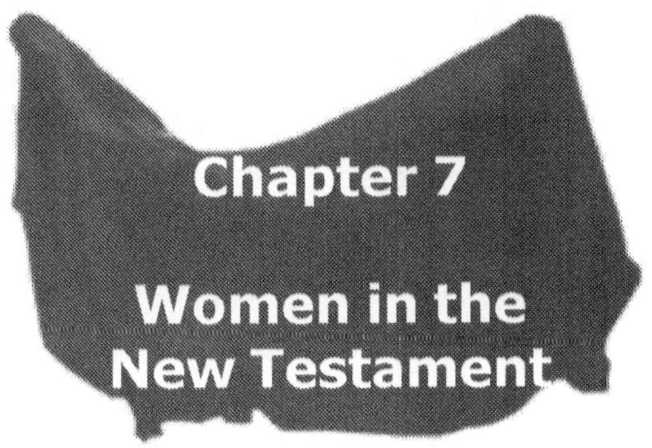

Chapter 7

Women in the New Testament

Women at the beginning of the New Testament era were, for the most part, seen as property, especially in the Jewish patriarchal structure. They were trained in the care of home, children, and husband. Limited access to higher education, involvement in political matters, and participation in religious discussion effectively kept them bound to house and home. Witherington quotes from *Roman Women* by J. P. Balsdon that, "Complete equality of the sexes was never achieved in ancient Rome because of the survival long after it was out of date of a deep-rooted tradition that the exclusive sphere of a woman's activity was inside the home..."[1] And yet Professor Witherington's arguments in the book show that Rome was actually more liberal in its treatment of woman than most of the Mediterranean world.[2] But even in liberal Rome a male member of the family controlled the woman. She was "sold" into a marriage contract with a mate of her father's choosing, could not conduct personal business without a male guardian, and could not hold an elected position.

As society progressed and men became more sensitive to the roles of women, the "inferior" race was now seen as having feelings and possessing self-worth. Trombley tells us that although women began integrating as a vital part of society, the Jews, however, "stuck to their tribal customs while the rabbis vainly tried to make them scriptural."[3] And into this scene comes our Redeemer, sent to the lost sheep of Israel (Matt. 15:24), breaking traditions (John 8:1-11), changing paradigms (Matt. 5:28), restoring humanity's position (Gal. 3:13), bringing division (Luke 12:51), and in all ways teaching that God's Word is supreme above man's (Isa. 55:9). Jesus' attitude and treatment of women was contrary to custom, and markedly different than the rest of the men around Him. One example of how men viewed women occurs in Acts 12 where Luke relates Peter's miraculous rescue from prison. As soon as Peter is released, he heads for the home where his friends are gathered praying for his release.

Acts 12:13-15

And when he knocked at the gate of the porch, a maid named Rhoda came to answer.
And recognizing Peter's voice, in her joy she failed to open the gate, but ran in and told the people that Peter was standing before the porch gate.
They said to her, You are crazy! But she persistently *and* strongly *and* confidently affirmed that it was the truth. They said, It is his angel! (Amplified Bible)

Rhoda was confident of what she saw and heard but was discounted as mad or crazy. And even when she confidently persisted in her affirmation that Peter was at the gate, they still refused to believe her and decided it was an angel. There are many occasions in Scripture where women were the first to receive revelation of supernatural events and first chosen to bring the Good News. Their revelations impacted both men and women. And yet in many of those same Scriptures the men around Jesus for the most part dismissed the women's contributions.

Mary and Elizabeth

Mary and her cousin Elizabeth were the first human persons to receive divine revelation that the birth of the Messiah was imminent. Mary was the one chosen to begin the process of reversing the consequences of Adam and Eve's sin by bringing forth the promised seed.

Genesis 3:15

And I will put enmity
Between you and the woman,
And between your seed and her Seed;
He shall bruise your head,
And you shall bruise His heel.

These words were spoken to the serpent, the deceiver, and the one who would spend the next four thousand years attempting to stop "her Seed" from being born. The enemy hated God's special creation above all things and it seems he held a special animosity for the woman.

After all, it was from her that his destruction would finally come.

The fact that the angel came to Mary announcing that she was highly favored of God and that God was with her (Luke 1:28) flies in the face of tradition that viewed her as property — something to be bought, sold, and controlled. She had favor with almighty God and the Holy Spirit would overshadow her. According to Strong's Lexicon overshadowing comes from the Greek word eperchomai {ep-er'-khom-ahee} which means: of the Holy Spirit, descending and operating in one.[4] She was filled with the Spirit of God, indwelt by His presence, and carried the Son of God, the redeemer of all mankind, the "seed" that would bruise the head of the serpent. No man could fulfill the role that God gave to this precious young woman.

This is the initiation of the tradition breaking truths that Jesus would bring. Her situation was beyond any male paradigm. To be pregnant outside of wedlock brought a sentence of death. Joseph chose instead to accept her as if she were already his wife and, rather than death, selected divorce as a more compassionate resolution. Divorce! A *privilege* reserved only for males. Even today in the most conservative of Jewish tradition, a woman cannot be free of a mate who leaves her unless he chooses to give her a bill of divorcement. But divorce was not an option. Joseph would become the caregiver of the woman and the child she carried.

Mary, as the mother of the "seed", is a type of the ecclesia, the church. Spoken about in Scripture in the feminine, we see the church filled with the Spirit, bearing seed, producing fruit, and liberating humanity.

Elizabeth, upon greeting Mary, is also filled with the Spirit (Luke 1:41). She carried the forerunner, the one who would prepare the way of the Lord. Elizabeth shocks all her friends and neighbors when she overrides their choice of a name for the child. This is a mild scandal, but still tradition breaking. These two most blessed of women, both filled with the Spirit of God, had preeminence over the male figures in their lives. Joseph and Zechariah take back seats to their women and the roles assigned to them. There is little mention of either man after their initial introduction in the Gospels. Mary, however, is seen as having a place in Scripture up to and including the Lord's crucifixion. Although Jesus' genealogy is traced from Abraham to "Joseph the husband of Mary, of whom was born Jesus who is called Christ" (Matt. 1:16), we know His true genealogy was directly from the Holy Spirit. Luke even tells us that Jesus was "supposedly" the son of Joseph (Luke 3:21). This natural genealogy satisfied the Jewish requirement of tracing the seed through Abraham and David. But Luke traces it all the way back to Adam. <u>Matthew Henry's Commentary</u> declares why:

> His incarnation, that he should be *the seed of the woman,* the seed of *that* woman; therefore his genealogy (Lu. 3) goes so high as to show him to be the son of Adam, but God does the woman the honour to call him rather her seed, because she it was whom the devil had beguiled, and on whom Adam had laid the blame; herein God magnifies his grace, in that, though the woman was first in the transgression, yet she shall be saved *by* child-bearing (as some read

it), that is, by the promised seed who shall descend from her, 1 Tim. 2:15. He was likewise to be the seed of a woman only, of a virgin, that he might not be tainted with the corruption of our nature; he was sent forth, *made of a woman* (Gal. 4:4), that this promise might be fulfilled. It is a great encouragement to sinners that their Saviour *is the seed of the woman, bone of our bone,* Heb. 2:11, 14. Man is therefore sinful and unclean, because he is *born of a woman* (Job 25:4), and therefore *his days are full of trouble,* Job 14:1. But the seed of the woman was made sin and a curse for us, so saving us from both.[5]

Anna at the Temple (Luke 2:36-38)

Elizabeth, Mary, and Anna at the temple all prophesied about the mission of Jesus Christ. Although Simeon spoke to Mary and prophesied to her about Jesus saying:

Luke 2:34-35

Then Simeon blessed them, and said to Mary His mother, "Behold, this *Child* is destined for the fall and rising of many in Israel, and for a sign which will be spoken against "(yes, a sword will pierce through your own soul also), that the thoughts of many hearts may be revealed."

it was Anna who gave thanks to God and spoke about the child *to all who were looking forward to the redemption* of Jerusalem (Luke 2:38). She shared the good news about Christ's mission to all who would hear.

Jesus And Women

Mary Magdalene

In John 20 we find Mary Magdalene arriving at an empty tomb. When she goes back to tell the others, they come and find the burial clothes but no revelation of what had occurred was given them. The disciples returned to their homes, but Mary stayed behind. It was to her that Jesus appeared, showing Himself as the risen Savior. She was the first to see Him alive and the first to give *witness* that the prophecy was fulfilled. A witness is someone who gives testimony. She shared her experience – testified – to the group of disciples. This is no different than sharing a testimony, bringing the Good News, or imparting a revelation in the Church today.

The Samaritan Woman

In John 4, Jesus confronts a woman coming to a well in Samaria to fill her bucket with natural water. He offers her living water. This occasion in the Gospel of John is extremely enlightening in that it shows Jesus as the tradition breaker, the respecter of women, the forgiver of sins, the imparter of revelation, and the teacher of women as well as men. The woman is not a Jew, is an adulteress, and in her shameful state comes to the well at a time of day when there wouldn't be too many people there. Yet Jesus draws her out, ministers to her, teaches her about the nature of true worship, speaks into her life, and reveals to her the fact that He is the Messiah she has been waiting for. This is the "most extensive personal conversation Jesus ever had with any-one."[6]

All this *scandalous* behavior was conducted in broad daylight. It was scandalous in that day for many reasons. Jews did not associate with Samaritans (John 4:9); a Jewish Rabbi did not speak with women in public especially during the day; Samaritan's were considered by Jews to be unclean and, therefore, Jesus asking for a drink from her water pot and receiving one would have left Him, according to Jewish tradition, in an unclean state. But Jesus came to redeem all humankind – man, woman, Jew, Gentile. After this wonderful encounter, the woman went back into town telling all who would listen about the man she had met.

John 4:39

And many of the Samaritans of that city believed in Him because of the word of the woman who testified, "He told me all that I *ever* did."

Here is a non-Jewish, adulterous woman reveal-ing Christ to a city and many are saved because of her testimony. What a wonderful example of Jesus coming up against, revealing the ungodliness of, and breaking the tradition of not only racial prejudice, but gender preju-dice.

Mary and Martha

In Jesus' day, a woman's role was fulfilled prima-rily in the home. She was expected to wait on the guests, do the cooking, cleaning, etc. We see in Luke's Gospel,

Chapter 10, that Martha exemplified the woman's role. She busied herself with the preparations necessary to entertain her guests. But Mary chose to sit at the feet of Jesus and learn from the Teacher. Martha wanted Mary's help and besought Jesus to rebuke Mary and send her into the kitchen where "she belonged". Jesus' response was not only contrary to tradition, but He showed us that the better thing is to listen and learn. In a day when women were prohibited from formal education, this went against men's ideals and society's traditions.

Luke 10:40-42

But Martha was distracted with much serving, and she approached Him and said, "Lord, do You not care that my sister has left me to serve alone? Therefore tell her to help me." And Jesus answered and said to her, "Martha, Martha, you are worried and troubled about many things. "But one thing is needed, and Mary has chosen that good part, which will not be taken away from her."

Mary chose the good part, the part we all need – sitting at the feet of Jesus and receiving revelation of who His is, what He did, and who we now are in Him. This good part cannot be taken away from us just as the good part could not be taken from Mary.

Woman With Issue of Blood

The significance of this woman and her actions warranted her mention in three of the four Gospels – Luke 8:43-48, Mark 5:25-34, and Matthew 9:20-22. Here is a woman rejected as unclean because of a condition over which she has no control. Any contact with her would render a person unclean. The Mosaic Law was clear:

Leviticus 15:25-27

If a woman has a discharge of blood for many days, other than at the time of her *customary* impurity, or if it runs beyond her *usual time of* impurity, all the days of her unclean discharge shall be as the days of her *customary* impurity. She *shall be* unclean. 'Every bed on which she lies all the days of her discharge shall be to her as the bed of her impurity; and whatever she sits on shall be unclean, as the uncleanness of her impurity. 'Whoever touches those things shall be unclean; he shall wash his clothes and bathe in water, and be unclean until evening.'

She had spent all her money seeking a cure and was no better. Faith, however, propelled her to push beyond the law, push beyond her humiliation at her condition, and push beyond her fear of reprisal. She pushed through a crowd touching many people, focused on her only objective – touching Jesus' clothes. This is such a beautiful picture of Jesus redeeming all from the curse of the law. When He perceived that healing anointing had gone forth from Him, He asked who touched Him. His disciples seemed a little annoyed at the question, as it appeared they were just trying to keep Him from being crushed in the mob.

Mark 5:30-34

And Jesus, immediately knowing in Himself that power had gone out of Him, turned around in the crowd and said, "Who touched My clothes?" But His disciples said to Him, "You see the multitude thronging You, and You say, 'Who touched Me?'" And He looked around to see her who had done this thing. But the woman, fearing and trembling, knowing what had happened to her, came and fell down before Him and told Him the whole truth. And He said to her, "Daughter, your faith has made you well. Go in peace, and be healed of your affliction."

Jesus affirmed and liberated this woman, breaking with tradition, and showing that He is greater than the law. Charles Trombley says that Jesus, "commended her before the crowd. Her sickness had not rendered Him unclean nor had she broken God's law. In so doing He nullified the rabbinical law that menstruation was a curse from God because Eve sinned."[7]

Adulterous Woman

In John Chapter 8 a woman caught in the act of adultery was brought before Jesus in an attempt to trap Him. The Pharisees that brought her quoted the Law saying that Moses commanded such a woman be stoned. But when we study the Pentateuch, we only find mention of a man being stoned for adultery. But nowhere in this account is there mention of the man who was partner with the woman in this sin. He seems to be conspicuously absent and ignored. Jesus, however, acts with compassion toward the woman, challenging the men that brought the accusation, and offering forgiveness. Jesus goes further with this subject of adultery when He teaches in:

Matthew 5:27-28

"You have heard that it was said to those of old, 'You shall not commit adultery.' "But I say to you that whoever looks at a woman to lust for her has already committed adultery with her in his heart.

This saying not only goes against the Mosaic law by taking it to a higher standard, it goes against the tradition of the day that puts the blame for adultery squarely on the woman. She is the temptress and man is unable to withstand her wiles. Yet Jesus places the transgression within the heart of man. This is not to say that a woman cannot lust or commit adultery, she surely can. It does however fly in the face of the culture, tradition, and worldview of women, liberating them from the mistaken notion that she is the cause of man's downfall (as discussed in Chapter 3).

Others

There are many more examples of women with whom Jesus dealt in opposition to culture and tradition. Many were among His closest followers. We know that the 12 disciples were men, but what about the 70? To assume they were just men would do an injustice to the Word for it doesn't qualify the 70 as only men. We know that on the day of Pentecost women were in the upper room; women received the Holy Spirit; women spoke in other tongues; women declared the wonders of God (Acts 2:1-11).

Women stayed with Jesus in His last hours, watched Him being crucified, were the first to meet Him at His resurrection and carry the good news, and waited for His promise in the upper room.

Jesus touched, healed, and liberated women throughout His ministry on the earth. His compassion was continually expressed at the plight of women.

He restored the life of a widow's son (Luke 7) showing His concern for her situation. Culturally she would be without support having no male in the family. Jesus taught in His actions that we are to care for widows and orphans, not discard them.

He healed Peter's mother-in-law restoring her to wholeness. He not only drove out the disease, He restored her strength and she was able to rise up immediately and begin to wait on her guests. Witherington says that because Jesus released her from the grip of disease (evil), "she was now free to serve her liberator and others."[8] All this He did on the Sabbath. Just as the work of the Cross liberates all humankind who chooses to accept that work, those liberated are now free to serve their Master and others.

Jesus healed another woman on the Sabbath (Luke 13:10-17), calling her a "daughter of Abraham". This was scandalous to the Jews since only a circumcised male was a child of the Abrahamic covenant. Women could not be circumcised; therefore, they could not be part of the covenant. Not only did Jesus destroy this paradigm, but also He equalized the genders with the work of the Cross. Paul tells us in Romans:

Romans 2:28-29

For he is not a Jew who *is one* outwardly, nor *is* circumcision that which *is* outward in the flesh; but *he is* a Jew who *is one* inwardly; and circumcision *is that* of the heart, in the Spirit, not in the letter; whose praise *is* not from men but from God.

Since circumcision of the heart is a spiritual condition; it can be applied to both genders equally. Jesus repeatedly tore down the tradition of the oral law and brought all into the fullness of covenant relationship with Him.

Galatians 3:28

There is neither Jew nor Greek, there is neither slave nor free, there is neither male nor female; for you are all one in Christ Jesus.

Jesus ministers to Jewish women and to non-Jewish women alike. After delivering a woman's demon possessed daughter, Jesus calls the woman's faith great (Matt. 15:22-28). He raises Jairus' daughter from the dead (Mark 5), delivers Mary Magdalene from demons (Luke 8), honors Mary for anointing His body for burial in the face of indignation and persecution (Mark 14), and in all ways affirms, honors, and liberates women bringing them into an equality with men that had been previously prohibited.

Paul and Women

Paul also affirmed, honored, worked with, and traveled with women. He ministered with Priscilla and Aquilla, who trained Apollos more accurately in the Word of God. Whenever their names are mentioned, four out of six times Priscilla's name comes first. According to

Frank Viola this is "ancient shorthand signifying that Priscilla was more spiritually prominent. Also, the fact that her name appears first when she and her husband instructed Apollos indicates that she led in that exchange."[9] Priscilla teaching a man? So it would appear.

It was Paul who told Timothy that he could trust the faith that he got from two women, his mother and grandmother (2 Tim. 1:5). He commends a woman, Phebe, to the church at Rome as a minister of the Gospel (Romans 16:1-2). She held the same position as Stephen the martyr and Phillip the evangelist. The text also uses the word **prostatis** — she is an overseer — someone with stature, authority, and responsibility (Rom. 16:2). He also speaks of a woman, Junea, in Romans 16:7 who is an apostle. He mentions Mary, Tryphaena, Tryphosa and Persis, all laborers of the Gospel. In closing the Roman epistle, Paul sends greetings to ten other women. Many women were house church leaders including Chloe, Lydia, Nympha, and Priscilla. In 1 Timothy 5:9 Paul instructs Timothy on the treatment of widows, and which women to put on the payroll.

1 Timothy 5:9-10

> Sign some widows up for the special ministry of offering assistance. They will in turn receive support from the church. They must be over sixty, married only once, and have a reputation for helping out with children, strangers, tired Christians, the hurt and troubled. (The Message)

Paul is the one who breaks the rabbinic tradition in which he himself was raised and insists that women are to learn the Word of God, just like men, with humility of heart in full submission to the truth of Jesus Christ. Throughout Scripture we see the inspired Word liberating women and bringing equality to the genders. Women are not less in the sight of God than men, but equal, and there is no prohibition in Scripture for women to function as evangelists, pastors, teachers, prophets, apostles, or in any other way to serve mankind for the glory of God. Many have done so in the past, and many more will do so in the future.

Chapter Seven Notes

[1] Witherington, Ben III. Women in the Earliest Churches. (New York, NY: Cambridge University Press. 1988). p. 16.

[2] Witherington compares the roles of women in Greece, Macedonia, Asia Minor, Egypt, and Rome quite extensively in Women in the Earliest Churches.

[3] Trombley, Charles. Who Said Women Can't Teach? (South Plainfield, NJ: Bridge Publishing, Inc., 1985). p 43.

[4] Enhanced Strong's Lexicon, (Oak Harbor, WA: Logos Research Systems, Inc.) 1995.

[5] Henry, Matthew, Matthew Henry's Commentary on the Bible, (Peabody, MA: Hendrickson Publishers) 1997.

[6] Jacobs, Cindy. Women of Destiny. (Ventura, Calif.: Regal Books, 1998) p. 271.

[7] Trombley. p. 225.

[8] Witherington, Ben III. Women in the Ministry of Jesus. (New York, NY: Cambridge University Press. 1984, Reprinted 1994). p. 67.

[9] Viola, Frank. Now Concerning A Woman's Role In The Church. An Open Letter. p 8, Online. Internet 6 March 2002.

Throughout history there have always been fair-minded men, walking in the revelation of truth, supporting women in ministry, and attempting to overcome the prejudice born of the curse of Eve. It seems, however, that these men have been in the minority for most women ministers have experienced severe persecution and prejudice primarily from the male constituency. Despite this opposition, women have continued to impact the body of Christ, bringing forth revelation by the Spirit of the Lord, and pushing through to see Kingdom purposes advanced.

Teresa of Avila

Teresa of Avila, an infamous female mystic, lived in the 16th century and is best known for her reformation of the Carmelite sisterhood in Spain. Her writings inspired many as she taught on prayer being the way to our "inner castle" as she called the intimate place where we commune with the Spirit. Teresa continues to be studied in contemporary times as people hungry for more of God search out ways of finding Him. This controversial, yet passionate worker in the Kingdom was "declared a doctor of the church because of her reform efforts, the profundity of her writings about the spiritual life, and her dynamic faith and love."[1] A lover of Jesus, anointed by the Spirit, Teresa is still *teaching* us today – men and women alike.

Jeanne Guyon

Jeanne Guyon, one of the most widely studied mystics of the 17th century, impacted not only her generation, but her writings continue to impact Christians worldwide today. Raised in a strict Catholic family, she was taught the Word by her father. Her love for her Savior grew to such extent that she entered into communion with the Spirit in a way that few have been able to achieve. Once she began to teach her methods, however, persecution from the Catholic leadership landed her in prison more than once, and she was even betrayed by her own brother. Her release was secured when she recanted her theories. Even though she spent the last fifteen years in seclusion, men and women of faith continued to seek her out with a hunger to understand more of God and how to achieve intimacy with His Spirit. Today many men and women study Madam Guyon's writings, searching for revelation on fellowship in the Holy of Holies.

Maria Woodworth-Etter

Considered by some Christians as having the most powerful ministry in the 20th century, Maria Woodworth-Etter impacted the world for the Kingdom of God. Because of some erroneous teachings about women – that they cannot be anointed of God – her calling would be questioned. But she was, without a doubt, singled out and chosen for a work by the Spirit of God. Once she heard the call, she never compromised nor turned from her destiny. Roberts Liardon quotes her as writing, "I heard the voice of Jesus calling me to go out in the highways and hedges and gather in the lost sheep."[2] Maria ministered to hundreds of thousands, brought healing to thousands, and worked for unity in the body of Christ. Maria's focus was Jesus Christ and the manifestation of His power in her meetings. She believed all God anointed preaching should be demonstrated with the Spirit and power as Paul tells us. Consequently, the power of the Holy Spirit to save, heal, and deliver was always present when she opened her mouth to preach and teach the Word under the unction of the Holy Spirit.

Aimee Semple McPherson

Another controversial female evangelist was Aimee Semple McPherson. I have ministered in Four Square churches where some members of the leadership team felt it was inappropriate and contrary to Scripture for a woman to teach. And yet Mrs. McPherson founded this very denomination. Although her ministry was full of controversy, there is no doubt she was called and anointed of God. Experiencing overwhelming grief at an early age when her young husband died on the mission field, she left the evangelistic ministry. After remarrying, she ran from God. Her new husband preferred her to function in more "traditional" wifely duties. But Aimee's fight with God almost cost her life. She could no more deny the evangelistic purpose God had for her than she could choose to stop breathing. Upon reentering the ministry, Aimee moved in such anointing and power that the ministry became known for its miracles. The presence of God would confirm her preaching with signs following. A powerful evangelist, pastor, and founder of a denomination, "Aimee challenged the leadership ethics of her day and called the Church to spiritual maturity."[3]

Kathryn Kuhlman

Another contemporary female figure with tremendous impact on the body of Christ was Kathryn Kuhlman. In Jamie Buckingham's biography, *Daughter of Destiny*, he relates the story of an anointed, powerful woman of God who was a very real, human person. Kathryn made mistakes, hurt people who loved her, was betrayed by those she loved, was married, divorced, and died at an early age. Perhaps some of the prejudice and persecution she experienced as a woman minister contributed to the negative events in her life; we cannot know for sure. But persecuted she was! And through it all, during 50 years of ministry, "she may have personally witnessed to her Lord's love and power before 100,000,000 people."[4] Kathryn Kuhlman was anointed of God, intimate with the working of the Holy Spirit, and walked in His power. She brought freedom from mental, emotional, and physical bondage to millions and taught us to love and work with the Spirit of God.

Jackie Pullinger-To

Jackie Pullinger-To taught us how to demonstrate the love of Jesus rather than just telling people that He loved them. She ministered in Hong Kong in an area known as the Walled City, a filthy, secluded, dark place 30,000 to 60,000 people called home. It was rife with drugs, gambling, smuggling, pornography, and every kind of sin imaginable. Into this world of darkness, Jackie brought the light of the Gospel and the love of Jesus. In her realization that these poor, lost people could not relate to the love of a God they had never met, she moved from talking about Him to demonstrating Him. She helped obtain assistance and housing for the poor, worked diligently with the Holy Spirit to release drug addicts from their bondage, and in every way fulfilled the charge of God:

Isaiah 58:6-7

Is not this the kind of fasting I have chosen,
to loose the chains of injustice,
and untie the cords of the yoke,
to set the oppressed free
and break every yoke
is it not to share your food with the hungry,
and to provide the poor wanderer with shelter –
when you see the naked, to clothe him, and not to
turn away from your own flesh and blood? (NIV)

Other Anointed Women

Corrie ten Boom, having survived the ravages of the German concentration camps, lived to tell the world that her life was a demonstration of the love and forgiveness of Jesus Christ. She traveled for nearly 40 years sharing the truth of the Gospel, "that Jesus can turn loss into glory".

Dr. Fuchsia Pickett "obeyed the call of God when it was unheard of for a woman to stand in the pulpit."[6] A noted preacher and teacher of the Word of God, Dr. Pickett still travels the world bringing the Good News even though in her 80's.

Ruth Ward Heflin has earned her reward and is now enjoying being fulltime in the Glory that she taught about so passionately. A minister to kings, world leaders, and the simple folk, her prophetic insight and anointing have caused the path of many to be more directly focused on the Lord's intent for their lives. She spoke personally into our lives in 1996 and almost all she spoke to us by the Spirit of the Lord has come to pass. We've seen our destiny unfold just as she spoke it would by the Spirit of the Lord. Sister Heflin served as guest chaplain for the United States Congress and the Pennsylvania Senate and hosted two presidential inaugural prayer breakfasts. Her life touched millions as she answered the call of God to be an evangelist, pastor, and Bible teacher. She taught us how to praise until He drew us into worship, how to worship until the Glory came down, and how to stand in the Glory as God does the work of bringing in the harvest

Dr. Heidi Baker, along with her husband Roland, minister to the poorest nation in the world, Mozambique. She has told us that all her theology, all her education, all her degrees could not penetrate the need in that country — until she visited a church in Toronto, Canada where, it seemed, God was doing something spectacular.[7] After her first touch from God she returned to the poverty stricken, flood ravaged country of Mozambique where she has planted hundreds of churches, seen the dead raised, witnessed every kind of healing miracle, and been the recipient of many supernatural wonders. God has surely anointed this modern day *female* apostle for the work of the ministry.

These are just a few examples of the many hundreds of women that have impacted the world for the Kingdom of God. We can no more call them anointed of the devil, than we can dismiss their work. These women are testimony to the truth of the Gospel of Christ, the Good News that all are free in Christ, all are called to witness, all are called to be one with Him, and no distinction is made in His service as to female, male, Jew, Gentile, black, white, red, or yellow. For people that stand firmly on the premise that women are prohibited from teaching or having a leadership position in the church, these women and many others like them, are testimonies to the fallacy of that position. Whom God calls, He equips. Millions have not only been born into the Kingdom through the work of these courageous women, but many men and women have gone into the ministry themselves because of their anointed work.

God has always anointed women to serve in whatever capacity He chooses to fulfill His purpose in the earth. They have served as pastors, evangelists, teachers, apostles, prophets, and in all other ways served the Kingdom and our God. The world is more populated now than ever before with unsaved people needing Jesus Christ. The fullness of the body must be mobilized to reach the massive harvest that awaits. Men only make up a portion of the body; women and children make up the rest. If the women continue to be restricted in their function, prohibited from certain roles in the body, then part of the body is restrained, constrained, and bound. It is an impaired body and cannot function in its fullness. God demonstrated through Adam and Eve that we are to be one with Christ, working together for Kingdom purposes. We are the light of the world. For anyone to quench the light that shines in women is a perversion of truth and an injustice to that part of Christ's bride. It is time in God's history for the bride, composed of men and women, to remove the veil that keeps that light hidden. When we make the decision to stand up, no longer mired in tradition and powerlessness, our Redeemer will quickly remove the stone from the wells where the fullness of the harvest is waiting to come forth.

I wish to leave the women that read this book with the words of my personal heroine, Maria Woodworth-Etter, as quoted in Liardon's book. Receive it as a prayer that you will take up the challenge of overcoming tradition, throwing off the shackles of Pharisaical thinking, and take up the mantle that God is placing on you to move in the power of the Kingdom. Jesus, at the Cross of Calvary, removed the veil of separation. Whom the Son sets free is free indeed.

My dear sister in Christ, as you hear these words may the Spirit of Christ come upon you, and make you willing to do the work the Lord has assigned to you. It is high time for women to let their lights shine; to bring out their talents that have been hidden away rusting; and use them for the glory of God, and do with their might what their hands find to do, trusting God for strength. Who has said, "I will never leave you." Let us not plead weakness; God will use the weak things of the world to confound the wise. We are sons and daughters of the Most High God. Should we not honor our high calling and do all we can to save those who sit in the valley and shadow of death? Did He not send Moses, Aaron – *Miriam* to be your leaders? Barak dared not meet the enemy unless Deborah led the van. The Lord raised up men, women, and children of His own choosing – Hannah, Hulda, Anna, Phoebe, Narcissus, Tryphena, Persis, Julia, the Mary's and the sisters who co-labored with Paul. Is it less becoming for women to labor in Christ's kingdom and vineyard now than it was then?[8]

Chapter Eight Notes

[1] Broughton, Rosemary. Praying with Teresa of Avila. (Winona, MN, Saint Mary's Press, 1990), Back Cover.

[2] Liardon, Roberts. God's Generals. (Tulsa, Okla. Albury Publishing, 1996). p 47.

[3] IBID. p 251

[4] Buckingham, Jamie. Daughter of Destiny. (South Plainfield, New Jersey, Bridge publishing Inc., 1976). Back Cover.

[5] Goll, Michal Ann. Women on the Front Lines. (Shippensburg, PA, Destiny Image Publishers, Inc., 1999). p '124.

[6] Jacobs, Cindy. Women of Destiny. (Ventura, Calif.: Regal Books, 1998) p. 143.

[7] On January 20, 1994 a visitation of the Spirit of God began in a small church by the airport in Toronto. Since that time hundreds of thousands of people from around the world have come to receive a refreshing touch from God. This visitation, now called "The Father's Blessing" is still going on as of this writing.

[8] Liardon. P49.

RECOMMENDED READING

Bruce, F. F. *A Mind for What Matters Collected Essays.* Grand Rapids, MI: Wm. B. Eerdmans Publishing Co, 1990.

Clark, Jonas. *Governing Churches & Antioch Apostles.* Hallandale, FL: Spirit of Life Publishing, 2000.

Clark, Randy. *Power, Holiness, & Evangelism.* Shippensburg, PA: Destiny Image Publishers, Inc., 1999.

Eberle, Howard. *The Complete Wineskin.* Yakima, WA: Winepress Publishing, 1993.

Goll, Jim. *Father Forgive Us.* Shippensburg, PA: Destiny Image Publishers, Inc., 1999.

Goll, Michal Ann. *Women on the Front Lines.* Shippensburg, PA: Destiny Image Publishers, Inc., 1999.

Hansen, Jane. *Fashioned For Intimacy.* Ventura, Calif.: Regal Books, 1997.

Helland, Roger. *The Revived Church.* Kent, UK: Sovereign World, 1998.

Jacobs, Cindy. *Women of Destiny.* Ventura, Calif.: Regal Books, 1998.

Liardon, Roberts. *God's Generals.* Tulsa, Okla.: Albury Publishing, 1996.

Pinnock, Clark. *The Openness of God.* Downers Grove, IL; Intervarsity Press; 1994.

Tenny, Tommy. *The God-Catchers.* Nashville, TN: Thomas Nelson Publishers, 2000.

Tetlow, Elizabeth M. *Women and Ministry in the New Testament.* New York, NY: Paulist Press, 1980.

Trombley, Charles. *Who Said Women Can't Teach?* South Plainfield, NJ: Bridge Publlishing, Inc., 1985.

Viola, Frank. *ReThinking The Wineskin.* Brandon, FL: Present Testimony Ministry, 1998.

Now Concerning A Woman's Role In The Church. An Open Letter. Online.

Witherington, Ben III. *Women in the Earliest Churches.* New York, NY: Cambridge University Press. 1988.

Women in the Ministry of Jesus. New York, NY: Cambridge University Press, 1984, Reprinted 1994.